FIFTEEN

WATER

PROJECTS

ISBN: 9781694887931

FIFTEEN
WATER
PROJECTS

JUAN SANZ SANZ

Between 1983 and 1987, Juan Sanz Sanz (1943-2019), unveiled eighteen water and land use projects that he had been carefully preparing for years; All of them were sent to places that, according to their estimate, could be taken into account and valued.

From the long shadow cast over time, we can, today, in the 21st century, be aware that some of them were carried out.

Be that as it may, just a month ago the author died and today, in September 2019, in his memory, we present here, in book format, fifteen of his **WATER PROJECTS**, the other three are already printed separately and also available in digital format for a few days on Amazon.

Africa, America, Asia, Europe, India, East ..., all the places of the Planet were thoroughly studied by Juan Sanz Sanz, a self-taught lover of Geography and also of History, and of his observation and deep reflections on human needs and the use of Nature to try to alleviate the enormous deficits that were already unquestionable then, were born his works that he transmitted privately to Institutions, responsible for States and public figures that managed these problems.

BIOGRAPHY:

Self-taught, Juan Sanz Sanz (1943-2019), devoted himself, from early youth, to unravelling the problems posed by the readings of historical events narrated by the various authors who frequently diverged from each other.

Geography was one of his great hobbies and reason for fervent study, not existing on the planet place, no matter how remote it was, which had not been fully informed.

The attentive follow-up of the social and political reality in which its existence took place resulted in proposals for water use on three continents and each of the projects was sent in its day to the places that were most suitable for its achievement.

Languages - French, English, Italian, Portuguese and German, in addition to his own, Spanish - had no secrets for him and thus he could fully enjoy the Literature written in them, another hobby in which, As an enlightened man, he found his peers.

In the early youth the Spanish guitar and later the piano, were musical instruments to which he dedicated a great effort similar to the passion that Music awoke in him and thus, in maturity, with authentic devotion and delicacy he interpreted beautiful pieces of Bach, Chopin, Debussy and Beethoven who contributed a lot to make their days more human and the passage of time milder.

In addition to the Water Projects it leaves many literary works practically about to be edited, something that will be sought in the public light.

Author Page in Amazon:

https://www.amazon.com/author
/juansanzsanz

Author Page Smashwords:

https://www.smashwords.com/profile
/view/juansanzsanz

In memoriam

CONTENT:

Arabian Peninsula

1985

SYNOPSIS:

Arabia cannot develop its industry because it lacks water and cannot produce food and create a minimum agricultural base.

An industrial country can import most of the food it consumes, such as England a century ago (* XIX), or Singapore and Hong Kong today, but it cannot lack drinking water. This is a much more extreme situation yet. Thus, we find a closed economic cycle, even if the basic conditions for this are met.

In reality, it is the tragedy of many important mining centres, emerged in remote places, lacking almost everything and that could not develop the entire economic cycle.

The mere accumulation of capital generated by the exploitation of oil fields is not enough to develop the entire production cycle. Precisely this factor is missing water, without which there can be no industries, neither large cities develop, nor large quantities of food are harvested.

Then there is the paradoxical and, in some way, dangerous situation, that these large capitals, which are there, must be used somewhere, and this is done in industrialized countries, which have managed to develop the entire cycle of production. Therefore, these capitals serve mainly those countries, in which they produce.

Territory:

Upon entering the Baghdad plain, the Euphrates carries an average flow of 710 m3 / s and the Tigris of 1,340 m3 / s. That is, 1980 m3. Here the plain is only 30 meters above sea level.

The canal we propose could collect the waters of the Euphrates, diverting this river to the SE, instead of letting it join the Tigris and bordering the cliffs of Kuwayt and Al Hasa.

This channel could bring a flow of 500 m3 / s to the northern coast of Arabia. A 12-meter radius pipe would be enough to carry water, or 5 6-meter radius pipes, or 10 4 meter radius pipes.

In this way evaporation and, above all, the maintenance of a constant level would be avoided.

The channel, however, is cheaper and there is no need to cross any mountain range, although the intake in the river is quite low. But, here you don't need the water to grow, but for the industries and the supply of the cities.

Basically, it is about taking advantage of the waters of the Euphrates (Al Furat) and diverting them towards the North-West coast.

Considerations:

We see that the origin of a strong economic cycle is in the use of surpluses of basic economic activities. However, let us observe, however, a paradoxical fact: a country with a large mining-energy base, such as Arabia, which, due to certain inconveniences, fails to take off and follow this cycle (* 1985).

In Arabia, huge surpluses of hydrocarbons raise the formation of a huge mass of capital. But these gross capitals do not apply to the creation of a powerful basic industry. That is, they are gross capitals.

The general rule is not that agricultural or mining surpluses form capital directly, without more, but that these are formed from the manufacturing activity derived from them. This industrial activity, together with the good commercial situation, gives rise to the true accumulation of capital, not the false one, which is the one derived from surpluses with no more than basic products.

The handicap of Arabia is that it lacks water, it is a desert. Where to extract it?

Arabia cannot develop its industry because it lacks water and cannot produce food and create a minimum agricultural base.

An industrial country can import most of the food it consumes, such as England a century ago (* XIX), or Singapore and Hong Kong today, but it cannot lack drinking water. This is a much more extreme situation yet. Thus, we find a closed economic cycle, even if the basic conditions for this are met.

In reality, it is the tragedy of many important mining centres, emerged in remote places, lacking almost everything and that could not develop the entire economic cycle.

Then there is the paradoxical and, in some way, dangerous situation, that these large capitals, which are there, have to be used somewhere, and this is done in industrialized countries, which have managed to develop the entire cycle of production. Therefore, these capitals serve mainly those countries, in which they produce, leaving the owners of the capitals in the condition of mere lenders.

We already know that this is not completely so and that Riyad makes enormous financial efforts to transform, to try to follow the productive cycle. But it is in vain.

The infrastructures that are made there are at exorbitant prices and, therefore, onerous; They are an insufficient and unnecessary expense. I am not saying that they should not be done, but that doing them will not allow Arabia to continue the cycle. We have already indicated the cause before it is a desert.

If water could be taken to Arabia, the situation would change, because the territory would have the fundamental element it lacks. That is why we might think that the evils of Arabia would be solved by the diversion of the Chatt el Arab towards its territory, instead of letting the water of these rivers be lost, whose total flow is almost 2,000 m3 / s, (it is say, 710 m3 of the Euphrates and 1,240 m3 of the Tigris at the entrance of Baghdad).

The Arabs could finance in Iraq the use for irrigation of part of the waters of the Mesopotamian rivers, in exchange for their surpluses being diverted to the northern plains of the Peninsula. It is, without a doubt, a great project.

Proposal:

"January 5, 1985.

I submit for your consideration and that of your Government, a proposal concerning the use of the waters of the Euphrates River for the supply of cities and industries and the irrigation of the northern coast of the Arabian Peninsula.

It will allow me to present some general facts. The Euphrates carries in Ramadi, when entering the plain of Baghdad, a flow of 710 m3 / s on average, while the flow of the Tigris is 1,240 m3 / s. Most of the almost 2,000 m3 / s that run through both rivers are lost in the sea or evaporate in the extensive marshes that cover the lower part of Mesopotamia.

On the contrary, the Arabian Peninsula lacks rivers and is supplied with water exclusively with underground springs. The proposal that I allow myself to direct consists in joining both complementary factors. Arabia needs water that is miserably lost in the Khalij al Arabah and this water could be carried along the northern coast of the Peninsula through a canal, since no mountain obstacle prevents it. If it were possible to divert, in this way, a flow of 500 m3 / s that would supply the industrial zones and the cities and irrigate extensive vergeles, the Arab States of the Gulf would have a very solid economic base.

This base is currently lacking. It is precisely the lack of water that prevents an industrial development in line with its enormous energy resources. The lack of water prevents the benefits obtained from the oil fields from giving rise to a complete production cycle, which leads from the possession of these natural sources of wealth to the conversion into a large industrial, high-tech and self-sufficient country.

The mere accumulation of capital generated by the exploitation of oil fields is not enough to develop the entire production cycle. Precisely this factor is missing water, without which there can be no industries, neither large cities develop, nor large quantities of food are harvested. Hence, in my opinion, the economic development of Saudi Arabia and the other oil producing States of the Peninsula is limited, unable to take that step forward. I will be forgiven for exposing things so crudely, but the facts, in my opinion, are like that.

It is a colossal work. But what better inheritance can the Arab people be left than the superabundant supply of the coveted vital liquid? In addition, the wealth that is hidden in the oil fields is transitory, it will be depleted over the course of a few generations. On the other hand, water supply is an inexhaustible wealth, of infinitely superior value. Arab states could develop the entire production cycle;

Not only would they have water for their industries and cities, but they would produce much of the food they need, without having to buy them abroad.

Maybe these ideas are not new and have been raised. It is something that from far away Spain I cannot know. If it were not so, I would be very glad that they could be useful.

Juan Sanz Sanz"

Drainage and cultivation of the Swamps of the Lower Magdalena

1984

SYNOPSIS:

As is well known, the great Magdalena River forms a huge palm area, covered with marshes and fertile floods, when approaching the sea. It is an inland delta caused by the presence of a coastal mountain range, of low altitude, but sufficient to slow the speed of the river, causing, on the one hand, the flood and, on the other, the deposit of rich silts during a long geological period. This is the most extensive potentially usable region of Colombia and has more than 10 million hectares.

If the waters of the floods of the Magdalena, Cauca, César and San

Jorge rivers, and the great rains that fall in the region, had a better exit, with almost all probability the flooded regions would be dry and ready for cultivation.

To correct the causes that motivate the current flood, which render the land useless for cultivation, facilitating the outflow of water and exposing the soils, a drainage, deepening and expansion of the current channels would be necessary, lowering the level of the bed bottoms. The town of Mompos is located at a height above the sea of approximately 30 meters. There is sufficient level to carry out this operation.

Territory:

The powerful Magdalena, when approaching the mouth, finds its way semi-closed along the coastal chain. Among its waters, those of Cauca. Cesar and San Jorge and the great rains that fall on the region, there is an accumulation of water, an almost perennial flood.

The bottom Sinu river can serve as an example. It is surely the potentially richest Colombian region. Exceptionally fertile soils. Its extension is 600,000 hectares (6,000 km2), much larger than the valley of Cauca (400,000 hectares), San Jorge (200,000 hectares) and Bogotá (145,000 hectares). The fertile soil has an average thickness of 1.20 ms. Its average height is 20 meters above the sea. The river is born in the Nudo de Paramillo (3,950 m.). From the town of Tierra Alta (about 120 msm) to the sea it is navigable for 245 km. Its urban center is Monteria (250), on its banks and at 20 ms altitude. The department of Cordoba, of which it is capital, has 1 Mhb (* 1984) in 25,000 km2, with a high density of 40.

The upper part of the San Jorge Valley is also quite cultivated. They are also very rich lands. The bottom is covered with bogs.

What we propose is a vast drainage operation, by dredging and deepening the main river channels, particularly that of the Magdalena, to facilitate the spontaneous outflow of water.

Reclus says: "Between the mouth of the Cauca and San Jorge rivers and the Calamar dike, the first arm in which the delta opens, it carries all its flow collected in a single bed for 100 km."

The river is grouped in a single channel, behind the interior delta. The heights of 100 ms on one side and the other are at a distance of less than 25 km.

The Magdalena is stopped by the coastal foothills of the Andes, forming a large inland delta. This seemingly imperceptible crossing stops water flow, reduces its speed and causes flooding.

In the same way, the Danube also forms an interior delta, being stopped by the Dobrudja hills.

What the coastal hills do is not stop the river, but slow down its speed, causing a stagnation of the waters, an inland delta.

The Atrato River, 700 km., Crosses extremely rainy regions and its flow is 4.88 m3 / s. Due to its abundant flow, it has been the subject of canal projects.

The Magdalena is located in Neiva at an altitude of 472 ms. Until Puerto Barrio the decline is small, but not very navigable because of its low flow and narrowness. Only from Puerto Wilches, at the height of Bucaramanga, you can navigate at all times with ease. Their floods occur in April-May and September-November and then cover large areas. The lands of the low course are of great fertility.

Mompos is at 33 ms altitude. Barrancabermeja, at 111 ms; Girardot, at 326 ms.

The rains in the lower part are enormous: 3 ms in Barrancabermeja; 3'8 in Caceres - at the exit of Cauca to the low plain. But few in the coastal strip. Although they are still larger on the Pacific side, where they reach 10 ms at some point, with 7 in Quibdo and 6 in Buenaventura.

The Magdalena, like the Atrato, owes its great flow to the rains of the lower part. This lower part is a huge rainwater receptacle that falls right there. The waters do not fit in the channels and spread everywhere. It is a region of great natural fertility, where the silts of Magdalena, Cauca, San Jorge and Cesar are deposited.

The Plains of Colombia:

The slope of the Orinoco has 350,000 km2. It has almost 6 months of rain, but the permeability of the soil does not allow the predominance of the jungle and vast areas of herbaceous vegetation appear, apart from gallery forests. The important thing is that these lands do not have quaternary formations, recent floods and, therefore, have little agricultural value.

However, what matters is the soil decomposition process, which takes various forms. It seems that it depends on many factors, because the climatic ones are mixed with the geological ones. No fixed rules can be established and, therefore, the agricultural value of that region cannot be known a priori, but it should not be large when it has not been put into cultivation.

Colombia:

The waters stagnate in a territory for a perogrullesque reason: they have no way out. Therefore, a fertile region, if it is covered with swamps, can be exploited if it is possible to give enough water to the waters. The problem is that the

Magdalena has a good exit, because there is unevenness.

Mompos, in the center of the inland delta, is at an altitude of 33 meters, at a distance of 250 km from the sea, about 300 by the river. Having, then, a certain unevenness, the problem is to give access to the waters by opening the channels, expanding them. That is to say, to build an artificial estuary to the river, a male channel greater than the current one, that gives itself access to the waters.

This is a territory of recent floods, made by the river, extremely fertile. Its extension is between 8 and 10 million hectares. If rice were planted - here, there are no temperature problems - between 40 and 50 Mtn could be obtained. You could also obtain crops without interruption, because the rains are very large, apart from the river floods. In the region it rains a lot, although there is a dry season too.

The possibility consists in that: there is an unevenness, then it is enough to expand the water outlet. What things should be done?

First of all, give way to the waters.

1. Reopen the old mouth of the Magdalena mouth towards Cartagena, making it a great exit.

2. Expand and deepen the current riverbed. That is, place at a lower level.

Expand and deepen the channels; make them wider and deeper. It is a work of drainage, in soft lands, served by the means of transport that is the river. The lands extracted from the swamps, it is enough to leave them in the banks, to consolidate them, by means of artificial dikes.

On the other hand, it would be necessary to contain the rivers at the exit of the valleys. That is to say, to give exit to the waters and contain the avenues. This work does not seem excessively expensive. You don't have to build new channels; the riverbeds, expanding them, are enough for this.

PROPOSAL:

"As is known, the great Magdalena River forms a huge palm area, covered with marshes and fertile river floods, when approaching the sea. It is an inland delta caused by the presence of a coastal mountain range, of low altitude, but sufficient to slow down the speed of the river, causing, on the one hand, the flood and, on the other, the deposit of rich silts during a long geological period. This is the most extensive potentially usable region of Colombia and has more than 10 million hectares.

The proposal that I allow myself to present consists in correcting the causes that motivate the annual flood, which makes the land useless for cultivation, facilitating the exit of the waters and leaving the soil exposed. This would require a drainage operation, deepening and expanding the current channels. Lowering the level of the bottom of the beds. The town of Mompos is located at a height above the sea of approximately 30 meters. There is enough slope to carry out this operation.

If the waters of the floods of the Magdalena, Cauca, Cesar and San Jorge rivers, and the great rains that fall in the region, had a better exit, with almost all probability the flooded regions would be dry and ready for cultivation.

In my modest opinion, in the use of this alluvial territory, extremely fertile, is the future of Colombia. Its extension is between 8 and 10 million hectares. Isolated flood lands, through better water outflow, a harvest could be obtained during the rainy season. Once the rivers are channelled, once separated from the general plain, its waters could be used for irrigation during the dry season and, therefore, to obtain two annual crops. It could be cultivated continuously, in the manner of this Mediterranean valley in which I find myself.

Colombia, an admirable country, needs a firm agrarian base with which to meet the growing needs of a superabundant population (* 1984). Population growth is itself a good, but human ingenuity must prevent it from becoming a tare for States, generously satisfying the needs it poses. If the suggestion that I am

pleased to send you is feasible, I would be very glad that it would have been useful.
Yours sincerely.

Juan Sanz Sanz"

Plains of Bengala and the Brahmaputra River

SYNOPSIS:

If the Brahmaputra River could be stopped by long, low-altitude dikes that formed a water pond that contained the annual flow of the great river (approximately 300 cubic kilometres), this water could be used during the rainy season. the monsoons.

If 10,000 pounds per second (300 cubic kilometres per year) could be retained in this pond, an irrigation of one cubic meter per square meter, sufficient for a good complementary harvest, could be given to a formidable land extension: 300,000 square kilometres, 30 million hectares; that is, the whole of the low plains of Bengal, Bihar or Uttar Pradesh.

It is a considerable work - the retention of water and its distribution across the plain. But the results obtained would have exceptional value for the Indian Union and for Bangladesh.

<u>**Clarification:**</u>

After years of thorough studies, many calculations and checks, Juan Sanz Sanz (1943 - 2019), released in 1984, by mail, privately and personally, to the then Prime Minister of the Indian Union, a proposal he presented with the next title: IRRIGATION OF THE PLAINS OF BENGALA WITH WATERS OF THE BRAHMAPUTRA RIVER.

Unfortunately, the very cultured man who many would not hesitate to describe as a prototype of a person close to the Renaissance has just died, given the great amount of knowledge that he sought to enlarge throughout his existence.

The baggage that provided his wisdom, due to the depth of the immersion he did for decades in Geography and History, together with the careful observation of how much was happening in those years throughout the Planet, then gave the spoiled author the necessary impulse to develop his works.

It is good to remember again that we speak of 1984, then, just as in this 21st century, the word weighed heavily against him, always present in a hierarchical excess society: self-taught.

Now, his Water Projects are published for the first time, this one, without moving a comma of the content bequeathed by the author.

Territory and considerations:

The problem of Indian agriculture is that it needs higher yields over the same cultivated area. It is not the case of new countries, without colonizing in depth, where it is possible to put new extensions in cultivation. In the case of India, we are faced with an overpopulated territory everywhere, completely occupied, in which every inch of land that can be cultivated is used greedily. In India it is not possible to cultivate new territories. The purpose is to improve the yield of those currently grown. For this there are, in theory, several paths. But only one is essential in all cases: as much water as possible. India must get the most out of its hydraulic resources and, with that, get more crops and higher yields in each of them.

Indian agriculture depends on the monsoons, their abundance and regularity. Roughly, it is necessary to start from the principle that to increase the yield it is necessary to retain water from the rainy season to use it in the dry season. This principle is well known, but it must be applied in full. The Indian government, aware of this, is making a great effort to build dams everywhere. But these are generally local water retentions, which generally affect small regions. It is a price to face the great solutions, to take full advantage, not the local hydraulic resources, but the large ones, which can produce transformations in a large region.

The Brahmaputra River carries a flow of 1,500 m3 before leaving Tibet. It has a slow, horizontal course, until it enters the gorges. At that time it has a width of 550 ms. It makes its way between two peaks, one of 7.7.50 ms and another of 7.100 ms, only 18 kilometres apart. Its width is reduced to 50 ms. In a journey of 42 kilometres descends 059 meters, by means of jumps, nonvertical. In a 200-kilometer journey, between Pe and Kapu, it drops from 2,950 meters to 695, that is, 2.2.55 meters. This could be one of the great electric power stations in the World.

This great river can be closed at some point, since it is licking the mountains of the Assam and some hills advance from the Himalayas towards it, especially in the region of Goalpara. In front of this villa we observe a line of hills over 200 meters high, which is close to the Himalayas. Even so, across the river, there is a distance of quite a few kilometres. However, a large reservoir in altitude would not be necessary, but in extension.

The important thing is to retain the waters of the river, forming a large lake, very large, not too deep, at most 10 or 20 meters. This would require a different type of reservoir, long dock. Let's not forget that the Aswan dam, which is already old, almost twenty years old, is 3 kilometres long and 110 meters high. To retain the waters of the Brahmaputra, with its 130,000 m3 / s, a drop of a couple of dozen meters would suffice, and it would be possible based on an impermeable earth dam.

The New Cornellia Tallings dam, completed in 1973, has a volume of 209 million cubic meters. If this dike on the Brahmaputra had a height of

20 meters, a length of 20 kilometres, and a width of 500 meters - it is just to give us an idea - the result would be identical to that of the previous dam: 200 Mm3. In the previous era, the Fort Peck dike was the largest, completed in 1940, with a volume of 96 Mm3, and this is on the Missouri. In between, we find Tarbella's, in Pakistan, with 146 Mm3.

In such a large reservoir, evaporation losses would be considerable, but little in relation to the huge volume of water in the river, since it would have to form a pond for 300 or 400 km3, retaining water throughout the year. This point of Goalpara, if the map does not lie, seems like an appropriate site. It collects almost all of the rains and is almost at the entrance in Bengal, but in the territory of the Indian Union.

PROPOSAL:

"December 1984.

Dear Mr Prime Minister.

I am pleased to address you to submit to the Government of Bharat a proposal regarding the use of the waters of the Brahmaputra River in the irrigation of the Bengal plains.

As is known, the Brahmaputra river carries a large flow (12,000 cubic meters per second) and if it were possible to retain its waters before entering the Bengal plain, it could irrigate a very extensive territory during the dry season.

From far away Spain it is impossible for me to know the terrain in detail, but the observation of a 1 / 2,500,000 scale map shows that the valley narrows at the point where its course turns south looking for the Bangal Ki Khadi. This point is in

front of the cities of Goalpara and Jogighopa, where some hills cross much of the plain from North to South, approaching the Himalayas.

This is the suggestion that I allow myself to present to the Government that you preside over. If the Brahmaputra River could be stopped by long, low-altitude dikes that formed a water pond that contained the annual flow of the great river (approximately 300 cubic kilometres), this water could be used during the rainy season. the monsoons

If 10,000 pounds per second (300 cubic kilometres per year) could be retained in this pond, an irrigation of one cubic meter per square meter, sufficient for a good complementary harvest, could be given to a formidable land extension: 300,000 square kilometres, 30 million hectares; that is, the whole of the low plains of Bengal, Bihar or Uttar Pradesh.

It is a considerable work - the retention of water and its distribution across the plain. But the results obtained would have exceptional value for the Indian Union and for Bangladesh.

I am also aware of the political problem that this suggestion poses, having to flood the waters of the Brahmaputra a considerable area populated by Asames and Bengalis, given the subtle and exquisite balance that must be maintained between the States of the Union. But if the retention of the waters of the Brahmaputra were possible by the means that I suggest, this would bring a general benefit to the Hindu people and, perhaps, it would be possible to wipe away a large part of the food deficit and thus cope with the demands that It raises a population growth so pronounced.

In the hope that the ideas presented correspond to reality, I wish you the best successes in your

political management and send you
my best regards.

Juan Sanz Sanz."

The possible system Caspian Sea-Volga River-Black Sea

1985

SYNOPSIS:

What we propose is to maintain the current level of the Caspian, not through the waters of the Volga, but with those of the sea. To do this, we must put in communication El Negro and the Caspian, opening a channel through the 700 km isthmus of Manich.

Then the waters of the Volga, instead of being used to create the Caspian, could be used to irrigate the large alluvial regions, below the level of the seas, but above the Caspian coasts. The waters of the great river could be distributed to the right and left, giving irrigation to a region of 20 million hectares, 200,000 km2.

At the same time, the channel that would unite both seas would not only serve to replace the Volga in its mission of maintaining the Caspian, but would play the role of a navigation channel, since the slope between the Black and the Caspian is 30 meters, that in 700 km they have an average descent of 0.042 meters / km, that is to say, 0.42 meters every 10 kilometres. Approximately one meter every 23 km. The drop allows perfectly the existence of a navigation channel without exclusives of any kind.

<u>**Territory and considerations:**</u>

I will be allowed to present some general facts, not less well-known acquaintances.

The Volga River is the main tributary of the Caspian Sea and decisively contributes to maintaining the level of this inland sea, subject to strong evaporation. The Volga is necessary so that the Caspian does not disappear because it is reduced to some lakes in its southern part.

But the waters of the Volga would be useful to irrigate the great plain that borders the Caspian Sea by the North, alluvial, arid and uninhabited region.

The solution we propose is to replace the Volga River in the function of maintaining the existence of the Caspian Sea by a channel that joins the Azof Sea and, therefore, the general system of the seas of the

World, with the Caspian, along of Manich's depression. With this, the waters of the Volga would be free for a second and much more useful function: to irrigate the land that dominates with its channel on the northern shores of the Caspian Sea.

The distance between both seas is approximately 700 kilometres and the slope to be saved, 30 meters, more or less, which gives a result of 0.04 meters / kilometre, that is, 1 meter / 23 kilometres. An imperceptible slope, which would turn this channel into an exclusive waterway, into a marine channel. Through it, the same amount of water that the Volga now provides will enter the Caspian.

In this way, two benefits would be obtained: to dispose of the Volga waters to irrigate the bordering plains to its mouth and put in direct communication of the Caspian Sea with the general system of the seas.

The canal along Manich's depression would have to cross alluvial and flat soils and the slope that it would have to overcome is very small. The works consist of opening a large ditch, a huge gap, with the only condition of maintaining the slope pointed above one meter every 23 kilometres. It would be easy to give this channel enough depth so that large marine vessels of all species could circulate through it.

With the high summer temperatures of Central Asia, irrigated crops of short cycle, from the waters of the Volga, would be possible in an alluvial territory of 20 million hectares, capable of producing huge amounts of food and definitely solving the problem that the Soviet Union It has at this time.

The work is colossal, but Soviet engineering can do it. It is the results that matter and depending on them you have to measure the effort. The gap along the Manich depression is possible and with it the use of the waters of the largest European river to provide the Soviet state with a solid food base.

<u>Volume of Water</u>:

The volume of the Volga is about 7,000 m3 / s. It is the longest and largest river on the European continent, along with the Danube. Its length is 3,400 km. Provides an annual flow of 220 km3 to Caspian

The Caspian is by far the largest lake in the world, with 436,000 km2. Its level is 30 ms below the general of the seas.

The Volga is the main tributary of the Caspian, but there are other rivers: Terek, Kura, Kizil Ozen, Atrek, Ural.

The evaporation in the Caspian of 1 annual meter represents a loss of 330 km3. The Volga contributes 220 and the rest the 110 that are missing, and it seems that there is a balance between what the Caspian receives from its tributaries and what it loses by evaporation. Obviously, there is, since, otherwise, its level would change rapidly and the extent it occupies a lot in a few years.

The 2/3 of the water supply received by this sea comes from the Volga, which becomes essential for it to exist. The waters of the Volga are not usable for agriculture, since they are necessary to maintain the existence of the inland sea.

What we propose is to maintain the current level of the Caspian, not through the waters of the Volga, but with those of the sea. To do this, we must put in communication El Negro and the Caspian, opening a channel through the 700 km isthmus of Manich.

Then the waters of the Volga, instead of being used to create the Caspian, could be used for irrigation of large alluvial regions, below the level of the seas, but above the Caspian coast. The waters of the great river could be distributed to the right and left, giving irrigation to a region of 20 million hectares, 200,000 km2.

At the same time, the channel that would unite both seas would not only serve to replace the Volga in its mission of maintaining the Caspian, but would play the role of a navigation channel, since the slope between the Black and the Caspian is 30 meters, that in 700 km they have an average descent of 0.042 meters / km, that is to say, 0.42 meters every 10 kilometres. Approximately one meter every 23 km. The drop allows perfectly the existence of a navigation channel without exclusives of any kind.

The result would be, on the one hand, the cultivation of 20 million hectares on the Caspian margins. On the other, direct communication between this sea, without the Volga-

Don device, with the general system of the world's seas.

The only question is the climate of those territories. The average temperature in January is -8 and that of July from 20 to 24 degrees. It is a territory with conditions similar to that of the Great Chinese Plain. It is likely that the summer is shorter and the possibility of using less irrigation. In any case, summer temperatures are higher than those in Western Europe and completely arid.

In short: if irrigation is possible in this territory, the device, although very expensive, once established would produce extraordinary benefits. For example, planted with rice, at 5 Tm / ha, 100 Mtn of this cereal could be obtained with the irrigation of the Volga.

The Manich depression channel should only be a wide ditch of land - since it always goes from sea level down - with that constant slope of 0.042 meters / km.

Proposal:

"June 1985.

Your Excellency Lord:

I have allowed myself to address you to submit for the consideration of the Government of the Union of Soviet Socialist Republics the attached proposal, regarding the use of the Caspian-Rio Volga-Black Sea system, if it is useful.

If the assumptions contained in said proposal corresponded to reality and its execution were possible, a territory of 20 million hectares could be put into cultivation, capable of producing, for example, 60 million tons of corn or 100 million tons of rice.

In the hope that these suggestions are feasible, I wish you the best successes in your political management and send you my best regards.

Juan Sanz Sanz"

Ideas for a Chinese agriculture improvement project

1984

SYNOPSIS:

By containing the spring floods of the Yangtze, many flooded, lacustrine lands would be exposed, ready for cultivation, so that the territory that should be flooded in the Han Valley would be more than compensated.

If it were possible to bring the waters of the Yangtze to the Great Plain, the spring harvest could be helped by irrigation during the sowing and harvesting seasons, and the harvest would be improved and secured during the monsoon rains.

With this, almost all of the Great Plain, 35 million hectares, would provide two crops and a considerable increase in yields per hectare. I would stop depending on the whim of the rains.

In addition, when the Yangtze was regularized with the reservoir, the lower valley of the great river would receive much less water and large lake and swampy areas could be cultivated.

I am aware that the project is of colossal dimensions and demands an enormous human and economic effort. It is possible that there are other means of increasing the yields of the Chinese field sufficiently. What I do believe is that, if this project were feasible and could be implemented, the gigantic State I would have secured a very firm agrarian base.

Territory, population and considerations:

What is in China is to increase the productivity of its agriculture. A series of agronomic improvements have been made: fertilizers, selection of miles: that is, adaptation to what is called scientific agriculture. This has been achieved in 30 years (* 1984) to double production. But the population has grown at the same rate. The problem is this. It is necessary to carry out a radical transformation of Chinese agriculture to end this vicious circle. In turn, it is necessary to end the rapid growth of the population, not based on physiological restrictions, but by a change in the material situation. This increase in agricultural production, which ensures the food maintenance and some surpluses of industrial raw materials to market, can only come from the generalization of the risks, since with the current means it has reached the limit of the profitable. You can't increase production by that way. It is necessary to undertake a new one.

For this reason, the problem of communications of the Sechuan through the river, with the outside world, is a fictional issue. Without the regularization of the Yangtze, it is not possible to develop the risks and increase the productivity of Chinese agriculture to a superlative degree. The problem of the Sechuan is not very different from that of the Chensi, also very populated and far from the sea, without the river serving as an access road, since the Yellow is not navigable. All Chensi communications must be done by land. The Sechuan has a navigable river. But because of this factor, China's agronomic transformation will not stop.

After all, from Chungking to Shanghai there is the same distance as from Chicago to New York. When a very productive inland region is far from the coast, if it has a river transport system, this is undoubtedly the best, but its products can also be competitive and profitable if the transport is done by rail and road. The differences are not so big. The problem of the Sechuan is that it needs a good rail network to the sea. In addition, in several directions: 1, to Shangai, descending the valley; 2, towards Canton and the Gulf of Tonkin; 3, to Beijing, which is the only one it has today (* 1984).

The Chinese railway network has 50,000 km2, while that of India, 60,700; Bengal, 3,000 and Pakistan, 8,800 (* 1984).

It is necessary to contain the waters of the Yangtze during the rainy season for the dry season. For this, it is necessary to look for the Sechuan another communication system. If the waters of the great river are contained, these results would be obtained: 1, avoid flooding of the low plains; 2, have water for a second crop; 3, compensate for the irregularity of the rains; 4, have a large source of electrical energy. They are the transformations that we already pointed out with respect to other countries, specifically those of the Mekong.

This must be done because, at the price of leaving the Sechuan without its river communications - replacing them with other terrestrial ones - China can be finally resolved to solve its food problems. I think the choice is simple. There is no advantage without inconvenience, there is no good that by evil does not come. But, that subcontinent is not going to see a situation desperate for not sacrificing the small river advantage that the Sechuan has.

Own China has an extension of 3.5 Mkm2. The rest, up to 9.6 Mkm2, are the peripheral regions:

Manchuria, Mongolia, Sinkiang and Tibet. Manchuria has an extension of 1.3 Mkm2; Mongolia, 2.7; Sinkiang, 1.7 and Tibet, approximately 3 million.

The biggest problem this project has is frost in North China. From Beijing, in which the middle of the year has frosts, to Shanghai, with three months of frosts, it presents us with a serious problem, since the cold ones are always an inconvenience.

Low China is open to glacial winds, while Sechuan, protected by the Tsinling wall, has much warmer temperatures in winter, a Mediterranean climate. Only the southern coast, from the Formosa channel, has a similar climate.

An archaic shield sedimentary bucket extends between Nankin and Beijing. This is the region that should be tried to irrigate.

This region has a temperature similar to central Europe in winter. Therefore, the benefits of irrigation would be quite limited, since winter irrigation is not convenient.

The change, in summer it has a really warm climate, similar to that of the deserts. For 6 months in the North and 9 months in the South, irrigation agriculture is not possible. This is the first data to consider.

China receives enough water everywhere for rainfed agriculture. The country itself does not extend beyond the rainy regions. The 400 mm line of average rainfall is followed by the Great Wall.

Summer is the rainy season. The coincidence of heat and rainfall allows the expansion towards the N of tropical crops.

In Beijing it hardly rains from October to April.

In central China there is no really dry month, due to the winter rains produced by the polar front. In contrast, in southern China, the dry season is more than marked and it rains little from November to February.

The irregularity of the rains is remarkable. In Hong Kong, with an average of 2.1 m, minimums of 1.1 and maximums of 3.1 have been known.

In Beijing the irregularities are greater. In an average of 65 years before 1935, with an absolute average of 624 mm, there have been 4 years with more than 1 m, and many others with less than 300mm. June rains are vital for cereals, with a recorded average of 85 mm, but in that period, 26 June have received less than 50 mm and 5 of them, less than 10 mm. The rainiest month of July also has great contrasts. That is why northern China is frequently shaken by hunger and drought (* 1984).

With this summer climate, the crops are the same from Manchuria to Tonkin. That rice does not predominate in the great plain is not due to the temperature, but to the lack of rainfall and the permeability of the soils.

Cultivated fields occupy 27% of the extension of own China (less than a third). Perhaps in recent years, it has managed to expand the arable land.

In Chensi and Chansi, the cultivated area comprises 22%.

In the northern plain and in the Shantung, the cultivated area is

68%

In the Yangtse Valley, downstream of Ichang, the average density is extremely high.

In the Sechuan, 1/3 of the total is cultivated, with densities per cultivated space still greater.

Finally, only 18% is cultivated on the southern coast, but the density is the highest.

In South China only 7 to 10% of the total is grown.

South of Ngan Hoei, rice becomes the main crop: double or triple yields of those that produce the remaining cereals, and more regular. The climate allows to obtain two annual crops. Half of the Chinese lands allow two annual crops and this average is widely exceeded in the southern part.

A complementary project would be the use of the waters of Amarillo. It could be done by diverting the river from Lanchou to the Wei Valley and irrigate, in this way, the Chensi. Apparently, the river carries more water on this site, which is it is at the exit of the mountains, which at the mouth of the Great Plain. Water evaporates in its long arch through the desert. If this water, through a canal, passes to the neighboring Wei basin, it could be used more easily.

According to certain observations, Amarillo would have 1,500 m3 in the lower course, compared to 3,000 m3 in Lancheu. It is necessary to see why the Yellow has so much flow in its sources, since this region does not seem too rainy.

Logging barely exists. The Chinese cut down forests in times past to get firewood (I don't know if this situation has been rectified in recent decades. Nor do they take advantage of their mountains through grazing.

The Chengtu plain, the best irrigated in China, feeds at 1,000 hb / km2 (* 1984). Equal densities are found along the Yangtze. The highest population densities correspond to the coastal plain of this river; in an extension at least 80,000 km2, the density exceeds 550 and in many regions 1,000, especially on the island of Chongming, in the estuary. The small coastal plains of the southern coast are also extremely populated, as is the Canton Delta.

Rice is the main food production, with 148 Mtn in 1981, 135 in 1978, 85 Mtn in 1961. A growing pace.

Wheat, 57 Mtn in 1981, 44 in 1978 and 31 in 1961. It has also grown.

In the central region, winter wheat is grown, which is harvested in late spring and gives way to rice cultivation. Winter wheat is grown in the northern plains and spring wheat in the Chansi and Chensi plains. The yields were 20 years ago of 900 kg per hectare, compared to 2,500 of the rice.

Millet is more resistant to drought and produces higher yields than North-western wheat.

The kaoliang or sorghum is cultivated in the Great Plain and Manchuria.

Corn is grown everywhere.

Barley, in dry weather regions.

Sweet potatoes are grown everywhere, with yields of 8 to 9 tons / ha. In the N, too cold, yields to the potato. China is the world producer, with 117 Mtn in 1978. Only in the poorest regions is the potato the main food.

With all these cereals, porridge is made, which is the common food of the Chinese population.

To this are added vegetables: cabbage, sweet potato leaves. Fats are obtained from soybeans, cotton, mustard Soy leaves appear in all meals.

A first fact that is obvious is that Chinese land is almost completely used to feed the population. Chinese agriculture has a minimum quantity of products for export. Almost all its resources are necessary for subsistence.

Birds, eggs, meat, fish rarely appear on the table even though their cabin is, numerically, exceptional.

The lack of concrete information that we suffer in the West about this country prevents us from stepping on these problems with a firm footing and we have to make the study based on the data available, from the point of view of a Westerner.

Above all, what this study tries to specify is the effect it would have on the Chinese agriculture, as it is today, a similar hydraulic work, which would mean the irrigation of most of the Great Plain.

The Chinese use little help from animals in labour. Oxen, donkeys or mules work in the North; in the South oxen and buffalo.

The latest data on Chinese livestock (* 1984):

Cattle, 64 M, 1/20 people.

Goats, 82 M, 1/14 people.

Sheep, 105 M, 1/10 people.

Pigs, 310 M, 1 / 3.5 people.

Horses, 7 M, 1/157 people.

Donkeys, 12 M, 1/90 people.

We see that the quantities are high, but the proportions are very low. Buffalo statistics are missing. The number of working animals is very small in relation to the population. That's why almost all the work is done by hand.

Four large rivers are born in eastern Tibet: Seluan, Mekong, Yangtse and Huangho. On the bottom of the valleys of Bramaputra and the Iravadi penetrate the monsoons. It seems that the rainy winds that penetrate these low valleys continue their course northwards through the valleys of the Tibetan rivers. It is something I do not see explained. The Iravadi River, for example. It is born in very rainy mountains and covered with snow, but not excessively high. The great Himalayan chain is over; the valleys of the rivers focus directly towards that current of wet winds.

It is clear that the growth of Chinese agricultural production is due more than an expansion of crop extension, a modernization of agricultural techniques. With this, rice production has almost doubled in twenty years, but the population has also grown vertiginously. The yields of 20 years ago were very low: 1 tn / ha of wheat or sorghum; 2.5 of rice This improvement in quantity will be due to the generalization of the selected seeds and the introduction of fertilizers in large quantities. It is almost certain that the modernization of Chinese agriculture has been carried out almost to the end. In that sense, it is at a critical point because, to the progress that in its day meant the redistribution of the property, torn from the estates and cultivated in a community way, with which the productions were greatly improved, it has followed the introduction or generalization of modern agriculture, which has been a very important second step. Now it is necessary to give the third one: the generalization of irrigation, the maximum use of hydraulic resources. It is a race against time, against population growth. That is why it is not possible to stop; The third step must be taken.

The Great Plain.

It is a sinking basin formerly occupied by the sea, it has been filled by rivers. They are very low plains, close to sea level, very wet.

The rivers wander between swamps and old abandoned beds; they change frequently and flow into muddy coastlines that advance rapidly over the sea, on low, deserted and inhospitable coasts. The soil is generally very rich. The great fear of the peasants is the flood, the overabundance of water, which breaks the dikes and destroys the fields.

The province of Hopeh is, in fact, the Peh river basin, which collects the waters of a vast mountain front from the SE of Chansi to the regions east of Beijing. All the waters of the northern part pour together by Tientsin, instead of going to the Yellow. The rivers of the Chansi mountains pour north instead of going to the Amarillo, which is much closer, because the region of the bottom of the Yellow, the Po Hai, is lower than the banks of the great river. These rivers have a torrential regime and converge in the surroundings of Beijing. As the outflow of all these waters is so narrow, during the floods the water traces the river courses and destroys the dikes and crops.

The navigation is very painful in these rivers without slope, tortuous and destroyed by the mud. The entrance of the Peh or Bey (name according to the new spelling) is obstructed by a bar and the medium-sized ships have to anchor several kilometres from the coast. The mouth advances 100 meters a year. Peh is covered in ice from the end of November to the beginning of March. The coast is so flat that it cannot be seen from the point where the boats anchor. Not everything is yellow slime; There are sandy moors that cost a lot to fertilize. The land, nowadays, more than cultivated, is turned into a garden. Kaoliang, cotton and corn predominate; Little wheat and rice. Infinity of villages surrounded by willows and poplars.

Huang's exit from the mountains is quite difficult. The river has had to open a narrow passage, which hinders navigation, between cliffs of loes whose landslides obstruct the current, despite its speed. The few places where the river can be crossed has great importance in Chinese history; thus, the Tungkuan Gorge and the Mongtsin ford (in front of Lo Yang). Here the roads that united the two halves of the Great Plain met.

The river flowed, in the mid-millennium III, by arms, towards the Hopeh, partly following the course of the Wei, and flowed into the sea to the Pekin's That. The power of the mountain rivers forced the Huang to go increasingly east.

It is estimated that Huang draws 500 Mm3 of floods per year, compared to 212 in the Mississippi. After a flood, villages buried under 3 meters of floods have been seen. When at each flood the waters spread freely, the deposited silt raised the ground level. When the channel was imprisoned between dikes, the bed rose above the lands. Towards the fork of the old and the new bed, east of Kaifeng, the bottom of the channel rises 5 meters above the arable land. We can already understand the danger that such a current represents, whose floods reach 20,000 and 30,000 m3 periodically. These floods cover the plain of barren sands. If a gap is consolidated, the river takes a new course. The bed is too narrow and high and should be suppressed. To the South of the Yellow extends a flat region, of rambling rivers, swamps and whirlpools of dust. The waters of the southern part of the plain pour into the Huai, a river of great floods, which flows into a large lake, west of the Grand Canal. Huge polders extend to the sea, which on occasion have given way, flooding. Even to the north, villages take refuge on other trees or surrounded by dikes. In spite of its waterways and clayey lands, the southern country gives an impression of poverty. Towards the Haui is quite unpopulated.

The Yangtse.

The Red Basin of Sechuan owes this name to the intense eye colour of sandstones mixed with clays, with a thickness of 1,000 ms in the northern part and greater in the center. This formation extended over much of southern China, but is barely preserved more than here, being more protected from erosion. It is not a plain, but a circular peneplain of 200 km radius and an approximate extension of 150,000 km2. There is only one true plain, that of Chengtu, of 6,200 km2. The rest is a succession of hills and small saws that rise around 700 ms above the riverbeds. Where there are sandstones, it barely grows more than pine; where clays, the crops are ferocious.

In summer, all the depressions and plains that can be watered are covered with rice paddies. Rains occur in summer. In winter the atmosphere is foggy, with rare frosts and warmer than that of coastal China. The temperature rarely drops below -3. There is a dry season, winter, although very foggy.

The Yangtse and the Chengtu River - converge in Ipin and here the Min is much wider. The Min collects the heavy rains and snows of the Sechuan Alps. Chungking is located at the confluence of the Jialig, a river that comes from the Tsinling and whose high valley is the road to Chensi.

Chungking is approximately 200 meters above sea level and Ichang at 4 msm. Between these two cities there are about 800 km and there are almost a hundred rapids. The river narrows sometimes less than 100 meters; the depths of the channel reach 130 meters, forming dangerous eddies. In turn, tributaries pour huge masses of debris into the river or landslides occur on vertical slopes.

From Ichang to the sea there are still 1,700 km and the bed is only 40 meters above sea level. Little below, from Shashi, it is contained by dikes; if he did not have them, he would invade in summer more than 100 km on both sides.

When leaving the mountains, it has a width of 800 ms; at the confluence with the Han it has 2 km. The course wanders through innumerable meanders, between the walls of the dikes, which barely reveal the plain. Floods fertilize the fields every year. Large floods occur every eight or ten years, transforming the valley into an inland sea, despite the dikes. It seems that the Yangtze ran in other ages through a series of stepped lakes; the eldest, the one above, on the plains of Hupe-Huaan; another in

Kiangsi's; finally, another one near Nankin. Large lakes remain, which accompany the course of the river. Lacustrine depressions were partly filled by river sediments. Lake Tungting has 120 x 80 kilometres in summer and is then a sea of fearsome waves. In winter it comes to dry out almost completely and through it the Hunan rivers keep their course. The great flood of the Yangtse fills the depression to a height of 12 meters.

Another great lake is the Poyang, at the exit of the Kiangsi rivers, also on the southern bank of the Yangtse. When the flood occurs, heavy reeds pass over the bridges over the dry season canals. The shore moves 30 and 50 km from its winter shore. However, the Poyang is never completely dry, because it is separated from the Yangtse by a mountain range that borders the river, reaching the exit of the 780 ms lake between cliffs. It is a sinking basin. This lake receives all the waters of Kiangsi province and it is obvious that it should be eliminated, since it occupies very fertile lands.

The best step for the upper channel would be: Ichang, at the exit of the gorges: or, better, the neighboring port of Shashi. Then, trace the valley of they have up to Xianjian.

Then, it would go up the Tang Valley, which converges at this point, to the port of Nanyang, where the altitude barely exceeds 300 meters. Thus, one would enter the Great Plain. The Yellow River is less than 200 kilometres away.

In these low plains, the humus and silt provided by the floods supply the fertilizer. When the waters are removed, beans, cereals and, in higher ground, cotton are sown.

Better than the previous step, it would be another to the East, the problem in such a case is to open a channel wide enough, several kilometres wide and deep enough to maintain a constant flow, always at the same level. It is a colossal work, but not impossible. The canal should attack the hills near Wuhan, to the N of the big city. The second channel could follow the approximate course of the Grand Canal, but serving as a drainage to the plain, since it is now one of the causes of its bogging down.

The project basically consists of using the waters of the mighty Yangtse or Changjian, 600,000 km2, 60 million hectares for the irrigation of the Great Plain. This is the purpose, It is a huge extension. The biggest drawback is that the plain is cold in winter. Even so, you can get two crops, one in spring and one in summer.

In floods, the action of summer rains is combined with the melting of snow. In Chungking the waters descend in March to 0.20 ms, while they arrive in July and August to 22 meters. This in the high course.

In Ichan the waters rise at most 13 meters; in Wuhan, the same; in Wuhu, 8 meters. The river stretches across the plain. There is a first flood in April, due to the snow melting and the river level rises 3 or 4 meters. The rest of the flood is due to the monsoons.

It is navigable to Ipin, 2,850 kilometres from the sea. The rivers of the Sechuan are also navigable, although their waste is marked. In the gorges, the flood rises and falls sharply, as the rains flow arrives; It is not a constant flood. It frequently reaches between 18 and 30 meters in one night, reaching 45 meters above the minimum waters. The speed of the current is extraordinary and for this reason the navigation was suspended from July to September. The reeds took a month to go from Ichang to Chungking; Of every 10 boats, one was shipwrecked or had major breakdowns. Each stream must be traced with tow´s. In Ichang, 13,000 reeds were registered. Until 1914 steam navigation was not regularized; thus, ships of 1,000 in summer and 500 in winter could be used. The largest reeds displaced 130 tons. The vapours used 6 days for the rise and 2 for the descent. They can circulate 6 months, from the end of March to the end of November.

Further down, 2,000-3,000 tons arrive to Wuhan. The mobility of sandbanks slows the trip. A boat had to go ahead, checking the situation of the banks. Sometimes the boats were dry, waiting for the waters to rise. These inconveniences occur, above all, between Ichang and Wuhan. There are 1,000 kilometres from this city to Sahngai and can be followed by 15,000 tons of ships during the high waters and during the rest of the year the fumes of 5.5 ms of draft. But the whole course has to be marked and constantly explored. So, the Yangtze is a good waterway for times gone by, but not for now. On the other hand, this is the best-or less bad-way of communication that the Sechuan has, which produces countless light products of great value: silk, tea, opium. But those were other times. The Sechuan has the railroad to Sian and Beijing. The drawback of this project is that the waterway would have to be suppressed, unless a system of exclusives was established, which was perfectly feasible.

But if the water was diverted to the North, the channel would have little depth, although it could be improved, becoming a constant channel, since below it also has - or had - great inconveniences.

The flow of the river is 29,000 m3 on average and 60,000 floods although 18,000 are attributed to it in other places. The first figure is more moderate and surely more reliable.

Chungking is 165 meters high. Between Ichang and Chasi, its course is still slightly fitted. Between Hankeu or Wuhan and the sea the slope of the river is 14 mm / km, with 1,130 km distance; therefore, Wuhan is about 15 ms above the sea. So, it is an extremely low valley.

The Yangtze network has 45,000 km of waterways, thanks in part to the sampans, which demand only 30 cm deep.

In the middle basin of Yangtse only 15 or 20% of the territory is cultivated. In the alluvial region lives a hundred million people (* 1984) in 100,000 km2. The power of this region is determined because it obtains two annual crops; wheat in winter and spring and rice in summer.

The Sikiang River has a basin of 400,000 km2, an average flow of 9,000 m3, with floods reaching 60,000 and marked drainage. Thus, Wucheu, is 30 ms above the river in the estuary, while the flood floods it. It is navigable to Nanning, 670 km from Canton. It flows into a delta and the main exit is west of Macao.,

The southern part of the Great Plain, the Huai Basin has an insufficient drainage, due, in part, to the artificial dikes of the Imperial Great Canal.

The Great Plain has 325,000 km2. To this could be added 1000,000 km2 in the middle basin of the Yangtse, the 100,000 of the Chensi and possibly 200,000 in the Sechuan; let's put 100,000 for the Sechuan. Total, 600,000 km2, 60 million hectares. The cultivation of two crops could be ensured: one in spring and one in summer.

The problem is twofold: 1, ensure the drainage of the plains; 2, get your total irrigation. The rivers have sufficient flow and perhaps irrigation is the minor problem, as we see.

The rains in the Great Plain are 500 to 1,000 mm. Along the Yangtse the rains are from 1,000 to 1,500 mm. The rivers of the Kiangsu and the Hunan have in their southern half rainfall similar to the coast, between 2 and 3 ms. Therefore, a total rainfall of 1.5 m can be applied to the entire Yangtse Basin.

The great avenues of the middle basin of the Yangtze are produced, almost equally, by the main river and its tributaries in this part. Therefore, it is necessary to dominate the waters of these great rivers to obtain the two objectives that we indicated before: flood the plains and distribute the irrigation water. It is necessary that the transfer channel begins, not in the Yangtze, but in Lake Poyang, where the waters of the Kiangsi province are bogged down, where it rains a lot and direct the water towards the top of the valley, to collect the waters of the Tungting Lake, which in turn collects those of the Hunan. So, one once the rivers of the southern slope of the middle course are controlled, reach the region on the Yangtze. Once here, cross the flooded plain towards the NE, to the outskirts of Wuhan and here, after also collecting the waters of the Han River, attack the mountain ranges that separate the basin from the great river of the Yellow Plain.

The central problem is that Ichang is 40 msm and Shasi, from where the waterway should start, is about 30 msm. It would be necessary to know what part of the northern plain is below 30 ms. It is necessary to think that it is necessary to occupy all the plain and a good part of it has to be above this height. That is why we have to go back to the initial project: close the Yangtse to achieve an altitude of 100 ms, raising it and forming an artificial channel that maintains this level on the plain. This is a very serious problem in a rather rugged space such as the Yangtze Valley. There is no choice but to limit yourself to Tibetan and Sechuan waters.

Better solution would be to close the river, not in Ichang, but in Zhijiang, where it goes to the plain of Hupe. From here you must enter the Han Valley and attack the mountains. It is a very complicated device to solve because the water of the Sechuan is not so much, it is not enough.

Therefore, we must return to the primitive project: two channels.

You must give the idea, expose the need for the work to be done. The result is already known more than 30 million hectares in the Great Plain; 10 in the middle valley of the Yangtse; 10 in Chensi; 10, in the Sechuan. In total an integral use with 60 million hectares of reward. These 60 million hectares, if they were cultivated exclusively of rice, at a yield of 5 tons per hectare, would be 300 Mtn. Plus the other wheat crop, for example, at 2.5 tons / ha, would be 150 Mtn. In total, 450 Mtn of grain. Currently, China produces half of that amount. It must be remembered that it is a low, very low plain, which has been filled by the Yellow River and other rivers that come from the loess. Therefore, it must be assumed that a large part of the plain is at a very low altitude, since it is a low plain, of light materials, flooded, with hardly any slope. Therefore, the altitude of Ichang (40 ms) or Shasi (about 30 ms) would be enough, without the need to dam the river and obstruct navigation. The point at which the Yellow changes orientation - that is, flows into one or the other sea - is around Kaifeng. Beijing is on a plain at 50 ms altitude. According to Reclús the altitude of Beijing is 37 meters.

<u>The crops.</u>

Rice was previously limited to the South and the Sechuan and has spread through the center of the Yangtze Valley. In 10 years, production increased by 60% after the end of the civil war. In 1954, 200,000 km2 of rice was grown, producing 50 Mtn.

Rice cultivation moves north, while wheat does south. The alternation of one and the other occurs frequently. Winter wheat and rice in summer. Thus, they grew 30 years ago 22 Mha.

Corn tends to replace sorghum and millet in the places it occupied in the northern part.

Orange trees in the South, apple trees in the North.

A multitude of oilseeds are grown sesame, peanut, mustard, rapeseed.

Soybeans are grown in the best soils, if it doesn't rain too much. In 1954 4 Mha, 40,000 km2 were cultivated. Now produces 3 Mtn and in 1954, 1.4 Mtn.

Population.

The 1953 census threw 582 Mhb. That of 1982, 1,000 Mhb; the one of 1964, 695 Mhb. In thirty years, the population has grown by 85%.

In the middle of the 18th century it was 180 Mhb; at the end of the century, 300 Mhb. -this data is quite uncertain. In 1850 it was 440 Mhb, with a considerable decrease in the second half of the 19th. A strong rise around 1900 standing on the same of 1850. A strong depression in the early 20, when it is again 350 Mhb. It grows in the first half of the century and in 1940 it has 4,500 Million, despite civil wars (paradoxically, which would show that war is not the best method of lowering the population growth of the country; much more effective is the misery). From here the growth is vertiginous.

It gives the impression that the Chinese respond, in this sense, as a people, as a race, and see the best guarantee of collective survival in number, in being the most numerous people on Earth, approximately 22% of humans.

In the Great Plain there are very populated territories, but others that are barely. Loesch's soils contrast with other alkaline and sandy soils. In the Huai the same thing happens next to really be overcrowded regions, there are others almost deserted, in the swamps. The loess plateaus are not overly populated, partly because of the abruptness of the country and also because of the irregularity of the rains. In southern China there is oasis settlement.

The Winter.

The Asian anticyclone is the most powerful on the planet and its center, if located near the Baikallos, boreal winds predominate since September. The winds are constant, often cold. Navigation is difficult for sailboats. The wind direction is NO in the North and NE. India and the Sechuan are protected from these winds by mountain ranges and their climate is less severe. The environment is dry and clean, but the mists appear as soon as there is a variation in temperature. It is the time of the drought, although it also rains on the southern coasts. The contact of the polar front with the warm winds of the Pacific causes abundant winter rains in southern China and lower Yangtse.

The summer.

As of April, the SE wind prevails in Shanghai.

Three air masses advance over Indochina, the Bengali monsoon, over Burma; in the center the Malay monsoon, on Sumatra and Celebes, that arrives in China; to E, the tradeoff of the northern hemisphere.

A characteristic feature of these rains is their great variation from year to year. The provinces to the N of the Yangtse are subject to terrible droughts with their sequel to deaths and epidemics. Drought and flooding happen.

That is why it is necessary to replace, as far as possible, the unstable, albeit easy, rain mechanism with the insurance, albeit expensive, of the rivers. This is a fundamental need. It is not only the amount of food that can be obtained with the irrigation, but the security of the harvest sufficient, especially if the irrigation capacity of the rivers is not hurried, which do accuse the climatic variations, leaving a margin of difference , between years of high flow and those of less. Within this margin, we must try to speed up the irrigation possibilities of tropical countries in general.

What is certain is that the Yangtze, except as a means of communication, is useless. The regions that it crosses receive heavy rains in summer, which ensure good harvests where it can be grown, and winter rains that allow crops in that season, a double harvest. This is not the case of the Great Plain, which only receives rains during the summer and suffers a severe winter drought, which generally does not allow winter crops and a second harvest. This is the problem. It is necessary to take advantage of the waters of the Blue River, which serve only for circulation, and direct it to the northern lands, ensuring a good harvest in summer and a second harvest in winter, especially with irrigation in autumn and spring, when which the risks or the rains are essential for the winter crop cycle.

There are two complementary elements: a river whose waters, very abundant, are not necessary for the countries that it crosses, and a great plain that needs water for the maximum use of its agrarian possibilities, These two elements must be fitted and the result can be the provide the Chinese people with surplus means of food. They are two powerful complementary factors, each of which separately serves little and together they can bear an exceptional fruit. The union of the complementary is the essential principle of harmony.

In the middle valley of the Yangtse it rains a lot, but not too much: Shanghai, 1,150; Wuhan, 1,260; Ichang, 1,100; Chungking, 1,100. The 1,000 mm isohyets go from Tsinling to the sea, passing through South Shantung.

In the Great and Northern Great Plain, it rains everywhere less than

1,000 liters. But the swampy basin of the Huai River has less than that amount of rainfall. Tsingtao, 660: Paoting, at the foot of the Chansi Mountains, 500; Taiyuan, 370.

Rains vary everywhere from 1 to 3; if the average is 2, they frequently descend to 1 and increase to 3. Thus, Pekin has an average of 624, which becomes 300 some years and more than 1,000 in others.

In the southern part of the Great Plain the rains have an average that approaches 1,000 mm. In the central and northern part, these quantities are halved by a good part.

In Nankin, winter lasts from the end of November to the beginning of March, almost 4 months. Winter is the time when the average temperature is below 10 degrees. Wuhan and Chengtu have approximately the same regime.

In Beijing, winter includes from November to March, 5 months.

Tsingtao has approximately the same regime.

In tropical countries, when the rains cease, even if only 10 days, evaporation sweeps the crops. Without irrigation, crops are reduced to floodplains flooded by floodwaters. To defend against these intervals without rains in full agricultural cycle, it is estimated that 1m3 / s is needed in every 10 km2 cultivated, Despite the relative irregularity of rainfall, the loss of crops due to this cause is really notable in many places: it reaches the third part, while the crops that have irrigation hardly notice it.

Irrigation doubles the yield of Java rice paddies and improves product quality. In addition, substitution is possible of low yielding plants, such as millet, for richer crops such as rice, cane and wheat. Dry season crops consume less water than summer crops but have even more need for constant irrigation due to lack of rainfall.

Some cultivated plants are sown in autumn and collected in spring. The necessary humidity is facilitated by the last monsoon showers and by the reserves stored in the soil; in some places, because of the rains and winter dew. The yield of these crops varies considerably according to the duration, irrigation and temperatures of the dry season. And it also depends on the irrigation being more or less widespread.

In the N of the Hindustan one distinguishes clearly between the culture "jarif" (autumn) and the "rabi" (spring). Fall crops include rice, corn, millet legumes and cotton. With the exception of millet and peas, these species cannot withstand the gangnetic cold and give way to other more resistant plants: wheat, barley, clover, mustard, flax, opium poppy.

Cotton is sown almost exclusively as an annual plant and thus has been able to spread to regions subject to frost in winter. Its cultivation requires average temperatures of 15 to 18 degrees for 6 months; 25 degrees for 2 months and considerable humidity. You need deep soils, where moisture is retained. In the Hindustan the collection begins in January and lasts until April, having to start 4 or 5 times as it matures; Flowering begins in October.

Although the growth of Chinese food production has been considerable in recent years - for example, rice has gone from 85 to 148 Mtn. This growth, in fact, has been parallel to that of the population, so that country is found - at least as regards the great basic productions - in the same situation as then. It is likely that progress has been made in other aspects, in other crops, that have improved the diet of the Chinese. But Chinese productions, which have grown a lot, have done so at the pace of the population and not faster. This is a very important factor to consider when considering the need or not for Chinese agriculture to be improved.

One of the improvements that have been carried out with intensity after the civil wars has been to take advantage of the pastures of the low mountains. Indeed, until the middle of this century (* XX), the Chinese disdained livestock and devoted themselves exclusively to the exploitation of agricultural resources. The contrast between the alluvial plains and the mountains or hills, almost always devoid of forest, was impressive. The Chinese concentrate on agricultural land and completely abandon those lands where agriculture is not possible in their own way.

That is why much progress has been made in this regard, since the rainy climate, despite deforestation, must maintain rich pastures, grasslands, garrigue, in which livestock would yield strong yield. Thirty years ago, the production of meat for consumption was very low, a rare complement to plant food, while in 1981 it produced about 23 Mtn of meat, almost the same as the USA and much more than the USSR. It is the world's leading producer of eggs. In contrast, the dairy and cheese industry are underdeveloped. This indicates that it has passed from the stage of livestock as a working instrument to food farming. In this regard, a good step has been taken.

Rice, mulberry, cotton, tea crops require the participation of large families. That is some do light and heavy Works. This may be the reason for Chinese high birth. Children are needed for jobs. As soon as they become men, they become heads of families and leave the maternal. In this type of agriculture, child labour is not only usable, but essential. The children do a job that, in another case, a man would have to do, and its maintenance is much lighter. So, it is really a business for family heads to have children in abundance.

On this issue we should reflect when addressing the problem of birth control in tropical countries. The large family is a natural productive unit. Seniors and children complement each other; Children work since childhood. In an autonomous agricultural system - each family forms a cell, an individual atom - there are countless jobs to do and children, from a certain age, relieve the burden and perform jobs that would otherwise be done by a major. Thus, we see that in these countries there are many children, not for barbarism, but for interest.

In this way, contrary to what is believed, birth control is not so much a medical problem as it is an economic one. These issues are dealt with very frivolously. We, in the industrialized countries of the North, do not know these things, we have no clear ideas. Birth control can only come from a modification of economic structures. We see that the population, however miserably alive, knows how to avoid offspring when this is an unbearable burden - in this, the miserable societies and the opulent calls shake hands, the extremes come together. The Chinese revolution has not modified these basic structures of society, but quite the opposite, because the Chinese population has never grown as rapidly as in the last 35 years (* 1984).

The revolution has not modified that structure, but, on the contrary, has developed it, it has been based on it. Hence the vertiginous growth of the Chinese population, which has doubled in that space of time. Precisely the Chinese revolution has consisted, in this aspect, of harnessing the cohesive force of the family unit. That is, the Chinese communal system is based, in reality, on the family unit. Two elements against positions that complement each other. To change, the only measure would be to mechanize the Chinese field and provide enough profitability. To achieve it, it would be necessary to transform it into a commercial and not only subsistence agriculture.

The sea invaded most of what is now the Great Plain, but has almost completely disappeared from it, and only subsists in the Gulf of Chili. In the other points its basin has been filled by sediments from neighboring lands, floods that, deposited in a tectonic pit, form the fertile lands of Manchuria and the Great Plain.

The Great Plain is a sinking basin. They are plains very close to sea level and very humid. This would lead us to the conclusion that the intake of the Yangtze at Ichang (40 ms) would be sufficient to irrigate most of the Plain.

PROPOSAL:

"December 5. 1984.

I am pleased to address you, to submit for the consideration of the Government presiding over a proposal regarding the exhaustive use of the hydraulic resources of the Yangtze River in the irrigation of the Great Plain of North China, which I will briefly discuss.

As is known, the Yangtze River or Chanjiang is the fourth in the World for its flow, after the Amazon, the Congo River and the Río de la Plata. Next to it, to the North, lies the

Great Plain of Northern China, covered with rich floods, which is one of the largest agricultural spaces in the World. But between them is a mountain range, the Dabieshan, which almost completely separates these two complementary factors. The Yangtze River carries a lot of water and the Great Plain needs it, but the line of low saws separates them.

The Great Plain is subject to strong climatic oscillations, with excessive or insufficient rains, which is manifested in agricultural yields. If the water of the Yangtze were taken to the Great Plain, it could complement the action of the rains and subject it to an intensive, safe and constant cultivation.

The proposal that I allow myself to present to the Government of the Republic consists basically of retaining the waters of the Yangtze at the exit of the gorges, below Yichang, and deriving part of its waters through a channel of 5,000 cubic meters per second and at a level of 100 meters above the sea, to the valley of the Han River, to create in this valley a large reservoir with lands below 100 meters. From the reservoir of the Han Valley, the Dabieshan could be crossed through a gap near the Nan Yang Gate, at which point the Yellow River course is not too far away. The course of the Yellow River would serve to distribute the waters of the Yangtze throughout most of the Great Plain, as it is maintained at a higher height than this.

The great Yangzi reservoir would completely flood the gorges, turning them into a lake near the great city of Chungking. Since the average flow of the Yangtze in Yichang must be 10,000 cubic meters per second, if half were used for irrigation of the Great Plain, the other half could be used as the basis for an exclusive device, powered by the electrical energy of the dam, whereby river vessels would ascend and descend through them, overcoming the obstacle. Thus, the Sichuan not only would not be held incommunicado when the dike was built, but the navigation would improve significantly.

On the other hand, by containing the spring floods of the Yangtze, many flooded, lacustrine lands would be exposed, ready for cultivation, so that the territory that should be flooded in the Han Valley would be more than compensated.

If it were possible to bring the waters of the Yangtze to the Great Plain, the spring harvest could be helped by irrigation during the sowing and harvesting seasons, and the harvest would be improved and secured during the monsoon rains. With this, almost all of the Great Plain, 35 million hectares, it would provide two crops and a considerable increase in yields per hectare. I would stop depending on the whim of the rains.

In addition, when the Yangtze was regularized with the reservoir, the lower valley of the great river would receive much less water and large lake and swampy areas could be cultivated.

I am also aware that the project I suggest is of colossal dimensions and demands a huge human and economic effort. It is possible that there are other means of increasing the yields of the Chinese field sufficiently. What I do believe is that, if this project were feasible and could be put into practice, the gigantic state would have secured a very firm agrarian base.

However, the realization of such a great work would not surprise us at all from a town that has managed to complete collective tasks as colossal as the Great Wall, the Great Canal and, above all, the colonization of the great swamps that covered the low plains in ancient times.

In the hope that the ideas presented are useful, I send a cordial greeting.

Juan Sanz Sanz"

Drainage and cultivation of the Orinoco Delta

1984

SYNOPSIS:

Due to the horizontality of the plain and the overabundance of land, a huge waterway can be built, always on the 100-meter coast. If it was 1 km wide and the levees were 10 meters high on the bottom of the bed, it could output 10,000 m3, a much higher figure. But it could be perfectly 2 km or 3 km wide. The width does not matter. It is not a channel in peneplain territory, which must be narrowed.

On the contrary, in the middle of the horizontal plain, what matters is that the dikes are kept at a constant height and that the bottom of the bed maintains a minimum slope for the water to flow. In this sense, the work does not present any difficulties and is perfectly feasible.

With respect to the Orinoco, the problem is extremely simple: it is a colossal work, but the result is that which can be derived from the distribution of 5,000 m3 / s of water for irrigation. They are 100 million hectares; in reality, between 100 and 150. The region would become one of the great granaries of the World. In turn, it would be able to absorb large masses of population, relieving social tensions in the countries of the area. This region would have an exit to the sea directly, outside the mouth of the Orinoco. I would be in depression between mountains of Caracas and those of Cumana.

Territory:

The Orinoco Delta, between Boca de Manamo and Boca Grande, has about 18,000 km2, 1,800,000 hectares. Further west of the Manamo Arm there are other lowlands, which could be cultivated if the land had better drainage.

The flow of the Orinoco is 18,000 m3, with floods that surely exceed 40,000 m3.

The whole problem consists in separating the river from the Delta, avoiding the enormous discharge of water that floods it. For this, it is enough to isolate it by means of a dike along the Cano of Boca Grande.

The extension of this palustrine region reaches west to twice that of Delta itself. They are low plains that pour into the Delta. The problem is that there come the waters of a territory of a million square kilometres, which have an average contribution of 18,000 m3, with double floods.

If the fluvial floods of the Delta were separated, the existing channels would only have to evacuate the rains and the small rivers of the surroundings, but the great contribution would remain.

Project and considerations:

The basis of the project is the construction of a large canal from the streams of Maipures to the coast. There is an extremely difficult region and it is the crossing of the Plains themselves. It is a swampy, lakeside region during the rainy season. Although it remains at an altitude of 100 meters above the sea and makes a long detour, it must serve as a collector to the rising waters of the Andean rivers. It is a fairly complex device.

However, we have a precedent, which can serve as a model: the artificial channel of the Yellow River through the plain of North China.

Leave this river to the low plain to the mouth, it runs for 800 kilometres through a swampy region also during the monsoon era. The work we propose here would be of similar dimensions. It is not ground what is missing to draw a channel as wide as you want. It does not need to be excessively deep, although it could also be projected for maritime navigation to reach the Upper Orinoco, the Casiquiare and El Negro, through which the Amazonian system would also be at your disposal. Thus, the greatest inconvenience seen in the work is the size of the canal. But this does not have to be a work too perfect: a relatively consolidated dike is enough that through the plain serves as a channel to the waters of the high Orinoco collector of the Andean rivers. At the crossroads of the rivers, a water outlet system towards the lower courses of the Andean rivers and the lower Orinoco. The thing cannot be, theoretically, simpler. This channel does not have to have a large depth. Due to the horizontality of the plain and the overabundance of land, a huge waterway can be built, always on the 100-meter coast. If it was 1 km wide and the levees were 10 meters high on the bottom of the bed, it could output 10,000 m3, a much higher figure. But it could be perfectly 2 km or 3 km wide. The width does not matter. It is not a channel in peneplain territory, which must be narrowed.

On the contrary, in the middle of the horizontal plain, what matters is that the dikes are kept at a constant height and that the bottom of the bed maintains a minimum slope for the water to flow. In this sense, the work does not present any difficulties and is perfectly feasible.

With respect to the Orinoco, the problem is extremely simple: it is a colossal work, but the result is that which can be derived from the distribution of 5,000 m3 / s of water for irrigation. They are 100 million hectares; in reality, between 100 and 150. The region would become one of the great granaries of the World. In turn, it would be able to absorb large masses of population, relieving social tensions in the countries of the area. This region would have an exit to the sea directly, outside the mouth of the Orinoco. I would be in depression between the mountains of Caracas and those of Cumana.

However, the usefulness of these colossal projects, which can be attributed to a messianism that they do not claim to have, can be considered. We are far from many points of view, which aim to reduce politics to mere combinations to walk around the house and to the general questions of balance between the States, when there is absolutely no relationship between one thing and another. My opinion is that progress cannot be made as long as the underlying problems are not resolved, since the possible combinations are exhausted. The shortage, the lack of means of the States (* 1984), in relation to social needs, has pushed them into debt and current bankruptcy. How do you imagine that they will leave this situation? Yesterday (* 1984) Alfonsin said that his country will meet its financial obligations abroad without undermining material progress. It seems to me the sincere expression of a good desire. But you can't deal with all that, just like that, especially while maintaining a situation that is the same as what motivated you. It is a dead end, like it or not. And Argentina still has the means and can go ahead more easily than Brazil. But in Brazil what is going to happen? All the benefits of its economy, which should be devoted to the attention of social needs, will go to the payment of debts. But is Brazil in a position to do such a thing, with 130 million inhabitants (* 1984). How are you going to prevent a country like that from entering a conflicting dynamic, against which that of the state media may be insufficient? The bankruptcy of the State will bring that of society.

The waters of the Orinoco begin to rise in April and reach their maximum in August - we are in the northern hemisphere -, coinciding with the rainy season of the Plains. Ä maximum water height is 30 meters on average. Then the descent slowly begins to reach its lowest level in March and early April, with an average of 16 m. The difference between maximum and minimum is not noticeable, due to the constant flow of the Guayanese rivers. The average flow is 18,000 m3 / s. The speed is small, due to the weak slope.

In Port Ayacucho, the rains are 2.5 meters. In the plain of Casiquiare the rains are over 3 meters. In the plain of Casiquiare the rains are over 3 meters.

Puerto Ayacucho is the starting point for navigating the river. In front of Ciudad Bolívar, the river crosses rocky outcrops that reduce its width to 800 meters. Llanero rivers have a seasonal regime.

Its length is 2,060 km and the basin is 880,000 km2.

In the western plains the rains begin in mid-April with isolated showers, which increase in May and peak in June or July, then decrease to cease in November or December. During the rainy season the rivers overflow and almost completely cover the plain, of which only small elevations that go unnoticed stand out during the dry season; here people and livestock take refuge.

From December to April there is half a year of drought. During the rainy season the wind of the NO predominates, while in the dry they come from the NE.

The dominant vegetation is tropical grasses. In the dry season, the grasses are narrow, and the green colour disappears from the landscape.

Puerto Ayacucho is located at an altitude of 100 msm.

If the Orinoco were diverted at the exit of the streams, following a channel along the 100m coast, it would take a long detour to the foothills of the Mountain range of Merida. The canal would collect the waters in the Andean river estuary, creating a strip cultivated immediately below it. This channel could make its way directly towards the coast, entering the Unare valley. From the streams to the mouth of the Caribbean there are 1,000 kilometres in a straight line.

The Central Plains extend between the Cojedes and the Unare. The 100-meter line above sea level separates a northern portion of tertiary land formed mainly by gravels and sands, and a southern portion of quaternary sediments. This region of quaternary sediments, between the Orinoco and 100 msm, was perhaps what could be used.

The dominant wind is from the E., with average rains of 1,200 mm, which fall by 80% during the rainy season. High average temperatures and intense evaporation. The terrain is porous, and springs abound. Pastures wilt in the dry season. Perennial rivers have gallery-forests.

The Eastern Plains extend to the E of the line formed by the Unare and Suata rivers. In the western part there are extensive formations of tubular plateaus, that come down from the Cumana massif. They are tertiary sediments.

Quaternaries are further to E, on the slope of the Delta. Quaternary soils are sand, gravels and clays. The permeability of the soil is large and the water seeps quickly.

The Western Plains extend between the Sierra de Mérida and the Orinoco. The decline of the plain is very constant and the same everywhere; The rivers do not have a defined channel. Most of it floods during large floods.

In front of Cerro Duida (2,396), where the bifurcation of the Alto Orinoco takes place towards the Casiquiare and towards the lower Orinoco, the altitude of the channel is only 120 msm. Here the river has about 300 kilometres in a straight line.

Lower Orinoco:

The Delta is a large area of recent floods, which is about 200 km from E to O, and about 150 km on average from N to S, with a total area of 30,000 km2, 3 Mhas.

The problem is considerable. The flow of the river is 18,000 m3 / s, similar to that of the Mississipi, quite regular thanks to the Guayan rains.

First, the river should be separated from the plain, giving it a unique exit through the southernmost arm, which is the shortest. Isolating the river from the plain, it would be possible to free the territory from the flooding of the river. But the rains are huge and with them the flood is guaranteed, this territory looks a lot like the Irawadi Delta.

The matter is simple, if you want to take advantage of the territory. Simply build a large dike along the Rio Grande, the southern arm, almost 200 km long. The other main arms must be blinded, annulled. These are the Macareo, for the center of the delta, and that of Mánamo, by the western limit.

However, it would be necessary to know to what extent the flooding in the delta is caused by the river and not by the local rains, which are 3 ms in the coastal part and 2 in the interior. Very high rainfall, enough for the region, if it does not have spontaneous drainage, to get bogged down.

It would be necessary:

First, remove the flooding from the river, by means of dikes that imprison it to the sea.

Second, use the current channels to exit local rainwater.

In front of Ciudad Bolivar, the Orinoco has its last narrowing, between granite outcrops, of 800 ms. Ciudad Bolívar is about 350 kilometres from the Atlantic, and 150 kilometres from Barrancas, where the delta begins. Under the Ciudad Bolívar the great Caroni flows, whose course is, however, regularized by the Guri reservoir.

The sediment load carried by the river is estimated at 100 Mtn per year. The coastal marine current drags the limos towards the N, like those of the Amazon and other rivers of the Guayanas. The floods that are deposited in the delta make it advance 45 meters a year. The great contributions of sediments come from the llanero rivers, since the waters of the Orinoco become cloudy during their floods and are cleared in their estuaries.

The flood begins in April and peaks in August, in perfect correspondence with the llanero rivers. The height of the maximum waters is 30 ms and the minimum, 17, which is reached in March and the first half of April.

Ciudad Bolivar, at 54 msm, has annual rainfall of 1,022 mm and 85% of these rains fall in the rainy season, from March to October.

Proposal:

"December 1984.

I submit to the Government for consideration a proposal regarding the use of agricultural resources in the Orinoco Delta, which I will present synoptically.

They will allow me to present some general facts, well known. The Orinoco is one of the largest rivers on Earth, with an average contribution of 18,000 cubic meters per second and approximately twice as large. This flow is the result of rains in a territory that has almost one million square kilometres. Throughout the ages it has been forming a large Delta, of fertile alluvial soils, covered with swamps, whose length is 17,500 km2. The large river floods and the region's own rains keep the Delta in a state swampy, waterlogged. But the alluvial soils, very rich, contain enormous agricultural possibilities.

The proposal that I allow myself to present to the Government consists in separating the river from the rest of the Delta, through the construction of a dike that runs all the water from the Orinoco along the shortest path to the sea, that is, along the Rio Grande to the Boca Grande, closing the other two main exits, Macareo and Mánamo.

If all the Orinoco's water flowed through the Boca Grande, leaving the rest of the Delta out of its floods, the remaining arms would only have to give way to the considerable rains that fall into the Delta itself and to the contributions of the small surrounding rivers, with which the level of the waters of the Delta would go down and most of its lands would emerge completely, having a good natural drainage.

In this way Venezuela would gain a territory of 1,750,000 hectares of feral land, to which we would have to add the territories located west of the Canyo of Manamo, on the mainland, which are also affected by the general flood.

The rains are very large, enough for the most demanding tropical crops in water, such as rice. A territory of 2 million hectares, planted entirely with rice, can yield a crop of between 8 and 12 million tons. The waters of the Orinoco itself, once separated from the cultivated plain, could be used for irrigation during periods of drought, so that this territory of 2 million hectares could be cultivated continuously.

With this, Venezuela would have a very firm agricultural base and could fully support itself in the supply of food products.

This device is similar to that of the Irawadi River Delta, in Burma, where this great river is separated from the plain by dikes, while the rains that fall on the region are sufficient for cultivation,

Hoping that the ideas presented are useful, I send a cordial greeting.

Juan Sanz Sanz"

Partial desiccation and cultivation of the Lakes of Nicaragua

1983

SYNOPSIS:

PROJECT:

What is proposed in this study is to partially empty the lakes of Nicaragua, lowering its level to sea level by opening a simple gap in the isthmus that separates the largest lake from the Pacific Ocean. With this, most of the bottom land of these lakes, whose current level is several tens of meters above the sea. They would be exposed and could be put into cultivation. The extensions of lakes and swamps that could be cultivated by this simple procedure would total about 10,000 square kilometres, one million hectares.

<u>ONE</u>

The central problem of the matter is that Nicaragua needs a solid economic base and today it does not have it (* 1983). Lacking minerals, hydrocarbons, major manufacturing industries or agricultural raw materials to export in large numbers, Nicaragua is currently a state without a firm base. This economic base must be found in some way or the political system will evolve in the sense that corresponds to the economic and social situation. The economic situation of a country determines the social situation and this the politics. The political situation is not a simple consequence of the economic situation, but it is strongly cond Thus, economic conditions fatally predetermine the material framework in which society has to move, its limitations and its possibilities. Therefore, if a State does not have a firm economic base, it is difficult for its social institutions to be firm. Politics cannot work miracles. Democracy is inextricably linked to well-being; If democracy is subjected for some time to the onslaught of hardship and social struggle, it runs the risk of collapsing. Hence, the State that is based on the system of freedoms that is democracy, must first resolve something that gives other points of view may seem trivial: its survival. It is often believed that the political system is by itself a panacea. It's something that the Sandinistas are seeing today. The political harassment they have been suffering from abroad is not the worst of evils. Much worse is the economic situation in the country, which, if not overcome, will prevent democracy from consolidating and consolidating in Nicaragua.

TWO

Nicaragua is today a unique case in Latin America. The independence movements against the Spanish monarchy in the early nineteenth century brought the establishment of national republics. The foundation of these republics was liberal democracy, emerged in Europe around the bourgeoisie and in America to the landowning oligarchy. Hence the democratic movement in America is parallel to the European one but taking different forms. If the principles of the State were democratic, their conditioning was colonial. In this way, we see democracy in Latin America take more diverse forms, which change over time, and which range from the purest democratic regimes to the most radical oligarchies.

Nicaraguan democracy has emerged as the result of a popular movement of reaction against democracy of liberal origin, which had adopted the most extreme form of the oligarchy, which separates it from other Latin American democracies and, in principle, brings it closer to the foundations of democratic socialism, emerged in Europe at the beginning of the second half of the twentieth century. Hence, this collective popular substrate, which is the basis of democratic socialism, is also the basis of communist socialism, and between these two possibilities the Nicaraguan regime has been found. There is no doubt that the support of the democratic socialist parties to this country can cause the political system to be firmly installed in it.

However, the future of Nicaragua is not played only in the fact that a genuine democratic socialism is established there, that external isolation is overcome and that those who are suspicious of the survival of the Sandinista regime end up supporting it. All this, being important, is not definitive, because the establishment of this democratic socialism would collapse if the country does not have a material basis on which to sustain itself.

THREE

What is proposed in this study is to partially empty the lakes of Nicaragua, lowering its level to sea level by opening a simple gap in the isthmus that separates the largest lake from the Pacific Ocean. With this, most of the bottom land of these lakes, whose current level is several tens of meters above the sea. They would be exposed and could be put into cultivation. The extensions of lakes and swamps that could be cultivated by this simple procedure would total about 10,000 square kilometres, one million hectares.

For a country whose arable land does not exceed 7,000 square kilometres, - a figure a few years ago - it is a considerable addition to their livelihoods. This million hectares of easy colonization, presumably fertile, of intensive use, would not only solve the problem of the lack of food that the country is suffering today (* 1983), but also have them to spare, whose sale could be the economic base on which to sustain the Nicaraguan State of the future.

To the benefits of taking advantage of new arable land, it would be necessary to add its intensive exploitation not only of rain crops, but of irrigated crops in the dry season, with which the yields could double. This would require a second phase of agrarian transformation, here already with large investments, which would have to be taken out, of the benefits of the cultivation, without more, of the lake territory today wasted. Some rivers of the Central American Andes, which all pour into the Caribbean, and lead that water to the cultivated plain, would have to be captured. This project would require large capital investments, as artificial reservoirs and canals must be built.

Recall that the headwaters of the Atlantic rivers, drained in other geological ages to the Pacific and were captured by the greater power of the tributaries of the other ocean. It would only be to make the waters return to their channel.

<u>FOUR</u>

On the economic base that represents having a million hectares of additional fertile land and abundant agricultural productions to export, a cycle opposite to the one that dominates the country would begin today (* 1983) Things do not remain static: or progress or recede. If you are not in the cycle of well-being, you are in the cycle of hardship. The lack of food and a firm economic base inevitably results in the cycle of misery and social dissolution.

Having a stable economic base creates a dynamic of progress and democratic consolidation. And, thus, gradually and slowly, over the years, of the elementary use of the lake bottom, it would be doubled through irrigation, thanks to hydraulic works that the same wealth could afford in the long term.

FIVE

The author of the study must state that he has reached these conclusions by having rather rudimentary means, that he has not studied the problem on the ground, nor can he determine many details that are beyond the information he has available. Some details or elements of judgment may have such importance, that they throw down the project. It is a risk to be taken. The specialists must determine their viability. I just limit myself to pointing out one possibility, which may be worth studying.

The most serious of the doubts that are raised to me - and it must be said from the beginning - is whether the bottom of the lake is fertile or not, if the extent of land that would be exposed once its level was reduced to that of the sea would be large or little. With the means I have at hand impossible to know. It can be assumed that the bottom of the lake is quite flat in the eastern part and deeper in the western part, towards the volcanic mountain range and the island of Ometepe. In the case of Lake Managua there is less doubt: all of it is above sea level and, therefore, would be dried up. In the case of the large lake, the extension of land that will remain above the level of the sea

I cannot determine it, but it must be at least 2/3 parts. It is a simple hypothesis or, rather, a good desire.

You can only carry out the reduction of the lake to sea level, because emptying the whole, leaving a part under it, would require such a drainage effort that would not compensate for the wealth obtained, at least for the moment, apart from the fact that have costly drainage works, which in principle should be avoided, since the work is intended to have a low cost.

In addition, the maintenance of this part of the lake at sea level is necessary for the development of another possibility we will discuss later.

SIX

This is the device of the lakes. A smaller, superior lake, whose surface is 40 meters above the sea, with a maximum depth of 20 meters;

therefore, all its aquatic mass above sea level. A lower lake, much larger, towards which the other one pours seasonally, at a level of 32 or 33 meters above the ocean, with depths that exceed 80 meters in some places; therefore 50 meters below sea level. In turn, the main lake pours its surplus waters along the San Juan river, 200 kilometres, to the Caribbean. Between the Lake Maggiore and the Pacific there is an isthmus that is 21 kilometres at its narrowest point.

Here is the lowest interoceanic depression in Central America. The watershed in Panama is at its lowest point at 87 meters, which the canal lowered to 28; here only at 32, which is the lake level. On this principle it has been tried to build an interoceanic canal or passage since the same time that the New World was known to Europeans. The San Juan river is relatively navigable for small boats, the greater lake allows to advance almost a hundred kilometres in the isthmus and the distance between the lake and the Pacific is minimal. However, the lack of navigability of the San Juan River did not take advantage of these facilities.

In the hypothesis that water would be released from the lakes until its level matched that of the sea, the upper lake would be emptied entirely and the lower one for the most part. This would reveal land that today water, fresh, covers. Alluvial lands, without spontaneous vegetation, that would be quickly colonized and put into cultivation, as soon as they dried. The extension attributed to lakes varies from one author to another, due to changes in their level and the uncertainty of their banks. The figures given range from 9,000 to 11,000 square kilometres. This would be the land earned for cultivation, because, although the eastern shore would dry out when the water level dropped. a part would remain covered with water, possibly extensive marshes of

<u>SEVEN</u>

If the bottom of the lakes is really fertile, if by opening a simple gap in the isthmus, the lakes are emptied, if the extent of land that is uncovered is really most of what is now covered by the waters, there is no doubt that through this work Nicaragua would have some extensions of arable land immediately that will allow it to maintain itself as a State and subsist as a town.

In addition, this project does not respond to a mercantilist purpose of cultivating a territory, by force of large capitals, in order to produce certain products that the world market requires. This is how plantations have emerged tropical Nicaragua needs this solution or another equivalent to survive. This in a national project, that only a new people, and a new State, like the Nicaraguan after the civil war, can undertake. It is a collective task that must unite effort, placate quarrels, open the way to a better future and show the world that Nicaragua wants to live in peace and freedom.

Nicaragua is doomed to a sad fate if it does not solve its basic problems, because, as we indicated above, it is at the beginning of a cycle of hardship (* 1983). The acute political problems that surround it can be overcome, but not those that result from a serious lack of material means. Nicaragua does not produce enough food and the agricultural products that it markets abroad are not enough to compensate for the cost of food and other necessities that it must buy. On the contrary - and we insist on it again - if you manage to have super-abundant means food, would be at the beginning of a cycle of well-being.

EIGHT

The problem of Nicaragua, unfortunately, can be generalized to many States in this world of ours. Today we are in a delicate situation, as many states have lost the basis on which to stand. Driven by population growth, the overpopulation limit has long been exceeded. This factor does not depend on a fixed figure, but on the relationship between the media and basic needs. Most Third World countries - almost all in tropical areas - do not have sufficient means of subsistence. This is partially offset by the sale of certain raw materials - agricultural or industrial; but the fall in prices of these materials has left national economies in a precarious situation. In principle it tried to compensate with the acceptance of credits abroad, with the belief that the crisis was passing and that better times would come. But the crisis does not happen, but continues, since its cause lies precisely in these fundamental facts. Indeed, it is the lack of purchasing power of tropical countries, which make up 2/3 of the world's population, the main cause of the economic crisis. It is necessary to increase the purchasing power of these enormous masses if it is desired that the products of the industrialized countries have a way out and, thus, overcome the global economic crisis.

Capitalism should realize that. It is necessary to support the general economic growth and to forget, for some time, the businesses with great benefits, of colonial type, because the world market is saturated. It is necessary to take that step forward.

However, Nicaragua cannot be waiting for world capitalism to be convinced once and for all that this is necessary and collaborate in a change of situation. Nicaragua needs urgent solutions and this project set out above to duplicate its arable land could be one of them.

It will take a long time for capitalism to convince itself that the misery of tropical countries drags it and threatens to destroy it. But these countries need immediate solutions. Until that arrives, there will be an intermediate period of many years in which these problems could reach a really serious extreme, with a whole range of possibilities that are of concern. One of these possibilities, as time goes by, is those murderous wars, which have no other purpose of decimating the population and leaving room for those who remain. It is hard to have to say it, but it is only a perfectly feasible possibility. We well know that when men find no way out of a situation, they can't think of anything other than organizing a war. They know something about this in Central America, although war, by its nature extreme and traumatic, generally produces consequences that were not foreseen; the purpose and the result rarely coincide. As far as possible, these eventualities should be avoided, not with vain preaching, but with practical results.

NINE

The greatest practical difficulty involved in the project is the operation of opening a gap between the main lake and the Pacific Ocean, whereby the lakes empty to the general level of the seas. The minimum distance between the two masses is 21 kilometres. This gap or channel would have to have depth the difference in level between both liquid surfaces, plus sufficient depth so that, once at the same level the two, the drain of the interior towards the outside was ensured. To this we should add the height of the hills that separate them, a dozen meters only on some front. And so, the ditch would be 21 kilometres long as minimum, a depth of at least 50 meters in the watershed and a enough width to ensure the emptying of the lake in a reasonable time. It is about removing land and removing them from the new channel of exit of the lake. In principle it would not be necessary more than to open a river channel so that the lake was emptied. The construction of a proper canal, which consolidates the work, could be done later; In principle, and for the purpose pursued, a channel is not necessary. You have to leave the lake through a river channel that serves as a drain. And a rudimentary work, consisting only of separating land in a straight line, however long it may be, is within the means that it now has or can dispose of, with some help, the country. An engineering work would need capital that now does not exist. But Nicaraguans have only to build a river, wide and deep, to its lakes. Regarding Lake Managua, in order for it to pour entirely into Nicaragua, it would be necessary to deepen the Tipitapa River, which currently serves as a drain, but which seems to give many detours, or open a gap of about 20 kilometres in length. A few hundred excavators, whose cost is modest, would suffice to carry out the work. These machines would then serve to colonize the new cultivated land and, finally, would constitute the core of the farm machinery park, once the crop was organized.

TEN

In human history the work of drainage of the lakes has a great tradition, Thus, we find related to this fact something as important as the origin of Egyptian culture. Indeed, it was on the banks of the El Fayum depression, the former Moeris lake, where the first stable villages were formed, from which the evolution of this culture begins. Moeris Lake once covered almost all the depression, which is below sea level and is fed by an arm parallel to the

Nile, the Bahr Yusuf. The tenacious work of men reduced the extent of the lake and put its banks into cultivation. The swamps, lagoons and marshes that accompanied the course of the Nile that were perennially flooded after the avenues, had to be won by human effort. In later Mediterranean history there is a tradition of drainage of lakes and swamps, provided that this has been possible through a simple drain, since the ground at the bottom of the lakes is usually of great fertility.

The case most like that of the lakes of Nicaragua is that of Lake Copais, in Boeotia, drained at the end of the last century (XIX) and today rich well-stocked garden of Mediterranean crops. On the other hand, there are the lands that were occupied by lakes in recent geological times and that have served as a nucleus in historical times of important human groups. This is the case of Bogota, whose importance is determined by the fertility of its region, the rest of an old lake; the most notable case, if possible, is that of Mexico City, whose agricultural territory was slowly won to the lake, a part of which subsists today.

Mexico City was the metropolis of the entire country from the moment of European occupation thanks to the fertility of its surroundings.

ELEVEN

The lake of Nicaragua and its annex that of Managua are an exceptional case in terrestrial geography due to its extension, its mild and rainy climate, its elevation above sea level and its proximity to it, which allows the discovery of its bottom with ease, and also for its strategic position in world communications, In addition, the lake would maintain the lacustrine system, although very small.

If a part of the current lake remains, being in direct communication with the sea, fed, in turn, of abundant organic matter by the tributaries of the nearby mountains that would continue to pour into it, there could be a case similar to the Tonlé Sap of Cambodia, exceptional spontaneous fish farm. The mixed fresh and saltwater, the abundance of natural food, could give rise to a fish wealth, enhanced by the fact that there are very few ponds of this nature on the American Pacific coast.

TWELVE

Finally, the reduction of the level of Lake Nicaragua to the general level of the seas would lay the basis for another possibility, which not far away should be left aside: opening an interoceanic route at sea level.

We already saw that on the low level of the lake (32 meters) the possibility of a communication in past times was based, since the maximum height of the passage is precisely that of the lake. Recall that the lowest point of the Isthmus of Panama was 87 meters in the Paso de la Culebra before the works, which lowered it to 28. Now, the Panama Canal runs through an exceptional and very narrow gap. Unable to engineering the beginning of the century, lacking mechanical means, to open a passage at the level of the Ocean, it had to establish a complicated device of exclusive and artificial reservoirs to raise traffic up to 28 meters above sea level. There is a circumstance that the space in which the Canal is installed is so narrow, that transforming it into a sea-level road seems impracticable and the best would be build another step elsewhere. It could be in the same isthmus of Panama. But it could also be in the isthmus of Nicaragua, of less height than that, although longer. For the construction of an interoceanic route through the isthmus of Nicaragua, the lake, due to its altitude above the sea, is an obstacle; in the case that it was emptied, the only drawback would be its considerable length (almost 250 kilometres), but with the advantage that the excavation of the canal and the support would be easier than any that could be opened through the jungles of Panama . With the great mechanical means available today, this interoceanic thirst path could be as wide as desired; it would be a true marine strait, free navigation, such as the Bosphorus.

A channel could be built here that really corresponded to the needs of our time, once the natural obstacle that is today the lake of Nicaragua has been removed.

PROPOSAL:

"March 1983.

As a work in support of the tasks of that commission, I am pleased to send you a study on Nicaragua that, if the assumptions contained therein were true, would contribute significantly to alleviate the problems of that country.

In the hope that this project is really feasible, receive greetings.

Juan Sanz Sanz"

Plains of Bolivia and Lake Titicaca

1983

SYNOPSIS:

The main object of this project is the territory, already in the Amazonian slope, that forms the high part of the Madeira river basin. Here the rainfall is enough for the dry land cultivation, the vegetation does not usually have much power and its colonization is within the possible. They are the Plains of Mojos, horizontal alluvial plain between the Andes and the Brazilian archaic massif, whose limits are the Beni and Guapore rivers. These rivers, together with the Mother of God and the Mamore, form a fan that, when gathered, give rise to Madeira. The river makes its way laboriously through the massif of hard bottoms by means of streams and waterfalls. The copious rains do not have a sufficiently rapid exit, forming a vast surface of flood in which the fine sediments that starts from the mountains are deposited, creating a vast alluvial plain, rich and deep. Every year an area of 120,000 km2 is covered by the waters, which take too long to leave due to the extreme horizontality of the plain and the narrowing of the channels below. This drainage work is what the human industry should seek. With this, the vast region would be won for cultivation and Bolivia would have a more solid material base than its mines to sustain.

PROPOSAL:

IDEAS FOR A COLONIZATION PROJECT OF THE PLAINS OF BOLIVIA.

August 1983.

<u>One.</u>

The point is that Bolivian democracy was kidnapped, first, and restored and now placed in conditions of extreme precariousness. It needs to succeed, if it does not want to be crushed and destroyed. It is an extremely dramatic situation, in which a democratic government is forced to succeed, within a very short space of time, if it does not want to be destroyed. The room for maneuverer is very small, the situation does not allow radical changes and the possibilities that the incipient democracy has of getting out of the test are quite problematic.

The situation in Bolivia - and in so many countries - closely resembles a vicious circle, in which causes, and effects arise and occur, always giving the same results. Democracy has serious difficulties in taking root in the country because the conditions are, to a large extent, against. It is difficult for democracy to be sustained when the natural conditions for it do not exist. It is necessary that these conditions change, so that democracy is consolidated and has a firm basis on which to stand.

The only way to break the vicious circle is to introduce new elements into it. The conditions of Bolivian society are, more or less, the same as in the past. Only the last few months have changed politicians, with the establishment of a democratic regime and a socialist majority government. But the background has not varied substantially, and politics cannot work miracles; Its short-term transformation capacity is very limited. With the elements at stake, which are almost the same as in the past, the results cannot be very different. Therefore, it is necessary to introduce new elements into the game of factors of Bolivian society that radically modify its structure. This is the proposal offered in this study.

Two.

Bolivian history is linked in the past to Cerro del Potosí. Other countries in the Americas have had this mining character, but not to such an extreme extent. In other countries, although the mining element is the decisive one, there is a greater balance between agricultural production and mining production. What is proposed in this study is to modify the structure of Bolivian society, transforming it from mining to agrarian.

In mining societies, the most extreme phenomena of wild capitalism usually occur. The benefits are greater than in any other form of production and with smaller capital. They are farms that depend on chance, the chance finding of a deposit. And precisely because the benefit can be so great and its achievement so rare, that is why a peculiar feeling is unleashed, in some cases baptized with the name of

"Gold Rush", which destroys all the brakes and barriers, creating a very special type of social and labour relations. In this case, capitalism and greed go together. The perspective of a great benefit and the impunity that almost always remote and isolated location of the production centres gives, unleashes greed and, with it, the establishment of extreme economic and labour relations, that in other forms of production would be anomalous.

Bolivian society has lived under this situation. But, at the same time, the mines have forced the population of regions where human existence is little less than unsustainable. Without the mines, Bolivia would be nothing more than a Peruvian province, an extension of Cuzco. It is the agglomerations that have arisen around the mines that have allowed the Bolivian nation to exist.

However, Bolivia is no longer "worth a Potosi", using the current expression in the Spanish language. Its mineral wealth is residual. They are no longer its fabulous silver mines, support of European capitalism for centuries, the basis of its economy. In the remote hill of Argentina its prodigious take-off between the sixteenth and eighteenth centuries. Indeed, the inexhaustible metal supplies of silver they supplied a good part of the numeracy with which European capitalism could develop. And it is paradoxical that, once those mines are exhausted, it is the tares of the latter that have plunged the country into hardship and despair. Modern capitalism is, in large part, the son of that Argentinian site lost in the celestial deserts of the Bolivian puna and should not be forgotten. Without the overabundance of currency that the site contributed to providing, the European economy would have been extremely limited in its exchanges and progress would not have been what it was. They are things of the past; but the past is there, under our feet, even if we forget it.

<u>Three.</u>

In spite of this, the mining wealth, of other metals, remains the support of the nation, the basis that provokes the production process that sustains it. But this wealth, although large, is not enough. This insufficiency has manifested itself, in the first place, in its inability to generate an accumulation of capital with which Bolivian society could have progressed more rapidly in the past. During the colonial era that Argentine wealth was stolen without more benefit for the country than the diminished wages paid for deadly work. The country has been independent for a century and a half and the situation has changed, although only in part. In Bolivia the whole process of the production of its metal wealth is not developed, but only the beginning of it, the extractive phase. The consequence of this is that the benefits for the nation are very lean and the State has few resources for its support, becoming a weak and vulnerable State, subject to constant disturbances.

If this wealth were greater, the Bolivian State would have more resources to make the country progress. The situation is contrary to that of the South African Union, whose gold and diamond mines allow the State to have resources with which it can impose a social situation that would otherwise be impossible. And there is the paradox that, in the countries of Spanish-speaking America, there is a deep-rooted democratic feeling, penury prevents it from materializing in concrete political forms, since the state is weak and cannot transform society, while other states, which do not want to be democratic, can maintain an anomalous situation only because the resources available to the Mining wealth has become an easement; it cannot be dispensed with, but, at the same time, it does not provide sufficient resources for the country to progress. Proof of this is the situation suffered right now.

But this is not the most serious of the imbalances suffered by Bolivian society. Mining is almost exclusively the only source of wealth, while the country suffers a severe shortage of livelihoods, since it does not produce them because its agricultural resources are very underdeveloped are sufficient to impose it.

And this is what we intend to correct with the project that we present below.

<u>Four.</u>

In the South American continent, good working lands are scarce. A large part of it is occupied by the Amazon rainforest, on alluvial lands, but not very fertile, due to the constant washing of heavy rains. From North to South, the Andes mountain range fragments a part of the continent in watertight compartments. The only extensive regions that are currently cultivated are the Buenos Aires pampas and the São Paulo peneplains, where the two factors that generate agricultural activity meet: fertility and humidity.

Not by chance have the two large urban agglomerations of the continent: Buenos Aires and Sao Paulo. The remaining agricultural areas are scattered in isolated nuclei and of little extension. They give the continent that typical form of peripheral and discontinuous settlement. In the Río de la Plata basin, it is where there are greater areas of arable land, but only in the region around the estuary is there enough moisture for agriculture to be possible continuously; It is the Pampa itself. To the north of it, the Chaco receives insufficient rains. Only in the transition zone between the Amazonian and Platense slopes we find the two factors together - fertility and humidity - that allow the development of large-scale agriculture. This region is the one that interests and is in Bolivian territory.

Here there are physical conditions very similar to the Argentine Pampas.

The main object of this project is the territory, already in the Amazonian slope, that forms the high part of the Madeira river basin. Here the rainfall is sufficient for the dry land cultivation, the vegetation does not usually have much power and its colonization is within the possible. They are the Plains of Mojos, horizontal alluvial plain between the Andes and the Brazilian archaic massif, whose limits are the Beni and Guapore rivers.

These rivers, together with the Mother of God and the Mamore, form a fan that, when gathered, give rise to Madeira. The river makes its way laboriously through the massif of hard bottoms by means of streams and waterfalls. The copious rains do not have a sufficiently rapid exit, forming a vast surface of flood in which the fine sediments that starts from the mountains are deposited, creating a vast alluvial plain, rich and deep.

Every year an area of 120,000 km2 is covered by the waters, which take too long to leave due to the extreme horizontality of the plain and the narrowing of the channels below. This drainage work is what the human industry should seek. With this, the vast region would be won for cultivation and Bolivia would have a more solid material base than its mines to sustain.

Five.

The use of this fertile region is a drainage problem. The waters that descend from the Andes, the horizontality of the plain, the vegetation of the gallery-forests that follow the banks of the rivers and the "cachuelas" or waterfalls that dam the river courses below, all contribute to the region flood, first, and stay flooded longer than the natural. The drainage should consist of lowering the riverbeds to a level lower than that of the plain and expanding these channels to allow the water to flow more quickly. The town of Trinidad, capital of the department of Beni, is about 70 meters higher than the first streams. There is, therefore, a considerable unevenness that can be exploited. Probably, with a simple drainage operation, a good part of this alluvial plain would be out of the flood. From this base, the colonization of the territory, which could be completed in successive phases, should begin with the product of the cultivation of this first space rescued from the waters.

This silty and potentially agricultural region has been created by flooding. Indeed, when it is flooded, the waters stop, and the floods settle. It is necessary that now the human work annul the flood and take advantage of the fertility left by the Nature throughout the millennia. The floodplain extension is estimated at 120,000 km2 but the one that could be used for agriculture, it is impossible to know with the means at hand. In the worst case, it is a very large arable area, with many millions of hectares. In this region, rainfall is considerable, so that rain farming is assured, without the need for irrigation. On the other hand, there is no dry season; it rains in all seasons and crops could be obtained without interruption.

The execution of drainage and deforestation works that are necessary for the cultivation of this alluvial plain seem more difficult, at first glance, than they really are. With the great mechanical means available today, the work is not out of the question. Just put the machines to work. Thus, for example, the Bolivian army has in recent years endowed, it seems, with considerable mechanical means, which in part could be used for this purpose.

It is only a suggestion, but in this way this army would emulate the Roman, builder of roads, aqueducts and new cities in previously unpopulated territories. An army should not fight only against potential enemies from abroad but also, if necessary, against those enemies, much more fearsome, which are misery, mismanagement, backwardness and its aftermath, symbolized in the Apocalypse. These are the true enemies to be overcome.

Six.

On the other hand, the inadequacy of own resources has forced the Bolivian State, to meet basic needs, to look for loans abroad that it faces with great troubles and places it in a situation close to insolvency. These creditors could be an interested party in the execution of a project that, even in the medium term, ensures the effectiveness of their loans, now problematic. If this project is achievable, not only Bolivia would solve most of its problems, but its troubled creditors. Bolivian foreign debt equals or exceeds the annual output of its entire economy.

It is such a risky situation for the creditor as for the debtor and both must join their efforts in the realization of a project like this, which would solve most of their problems.

The cultivation of several million hectares of fertile land (there are 12 that cover the flood), would not only provide Bolivia with sufficient food and, in general, the satisfaction of the basic needs of its 6 million inhabitants, but also the most of the crop could be dedicated to commercial farms. Thus, cotton cultivation could give rise to the industrial cycle, and the cultivation of corn to the livestock cycle. All this, of course, in the long term, but on this basis. Bolivia could leave the minimum economic level that is the mere production of raw materials and reach a level similar to the current Brazilian and Argentine, intermediate between underdeveloped and industrial societies.

Seven.

After a first phase of use of this floodplain through simple drainage works and, on the wealth, generated, in the medium term a second phase of exhaustive use of the resources of the region could begin.

First, the Beni River is the most dangerous current. Limit this plain to the west. It is necessary to separate it from it, enclosing it between dikes.

The Amazon-Madeira river system could be, despite its length, an outlet for products and direct communication to the central Atlantic. The 10,000 tn vessels can go up the Madeira to Porto Velho, at the beginning of the waterfall section. In a stretch of 350 km, navigation is interrupted. It would be necessary to build a large reservoir in the vicinity of this city at 70 meters high, which would permanently flood the entire region of the falls and allow navigation on them. By means of exclusions one could ascend from the Madeira to the lake, forming a continuous navigation line. In addition, the flow of Madeira, which should be at this point of about 10,000 m3 / s would ensure the supply of energy to the region.

Finally, if the crops in the Plains of Mojos are possible with the constant rains of the region. The same does not happen with the arable land of the Plains of Chiquitos, to the Southeast of those, in a more arid region. Irrigation is needed here, and water could be taken from the Andean rivers from Beni to Mamore. If the Beni were dammed at the exit of the mountains and a channel was drafted by the foot of the mountains towards the South, collecting the waters of these minor tributaries, not only would the flooding of the plain be reduced, but this water would divert towards the Plains of Chiquitos, which could form a second colonization nucleus, this time by irrigation. With this and with the river communication with the Paraguay-Paraná system, the device would be concluded and the old dream of communicating the two great river transport systems of the Amazon and the Plate River would be culminated.

Correspondence:

"September 1986.

Your Excellency Lord:

I am pleased to address you to submit to the Government of the Republic of Bolivia a proposal concerning the agricultural use of the Lago-Titicaca-Río Desaguadero-Lago Poopo system, which, in short, consists in deepening the Desaguadero riverbed , facilitating the exit of the main lake. This would result in the following results:

1 By deepening a few tens of meters the bed of the Desaguadero river, a large part of the Titicaca extension would be emptied, so that the space - which is difficult from here to determine - would be available for cultivation, in a region where rainfall is enough.

2 By reducing the extent of the main lake (which would perhaps be converted into a group of smaller lakes), the evaporation that now occurs in it (more than one meter per year) would be reduced and there would be more fresh water, coming from the rivers that They feed the lake. Thus, the Desaguadero river would multiply its flow several times.

3 Said freshwater flow - around 500 meters3 / second could be used to irrigate the arid region near Lake Poopo. If it were necessary to dry out this lake, to cultivate its bottom, it would be enough to open the temporary channel of the Lacajahuira river, which flows into the Salar de Uyuni.

The difference in level between the highest and lowest lake deposits is approximately 150 meters. There seems to be enough room for manoeuvre to modify the current device for the benefit of the Bolivian Nation.

With an area of 300 or 500 meters3 / second, an area of several hundred thousand hectares can be irrigated, capable of providing large crops and considerably increasing the level and life of the Bolivian people.

Wishing you the best successes in your political management, you are greeted attentively.

Juan Sanz Sanz"

"November 1987.

Your Excellency, Ambassador:

I have the pleasure of sending you a photocopy of the letter addressed to His Excellency, President of the Republic in La Paz, asking for your kindness and attention, deign to initiate some steps if you deem appropriate, to try to know at what point is the proposal that It is contained in it.

I still have to bother His Excellency asking for his attention towards the nine-page attached study entitled "Ideas for a colonization project of the Plains of Bolivia", which I put to your guardianship if you deem it appropriate, is sent to your country, where Believes it convenient.

I must inform His Excellency that this study on Los Llanos has been found since I did it in 1983 at the United Nations as a cultural background.

I would not say goodbye to His Excellency without having thanked him in advance for his attention and asked to excuse for any inconvenience it may cause.

Receive a respectful greeting,

Juan Sanz Sanz"

Lake Victoria

1984

SYNOPSIS:

The proposal we have allowed ourselves to make is the following. Due to its altitude and the rapid descent that follows, the Nile Victoria could easily be emptied, deepening the Nile channel a few tens of meters. Thus, almost all the surface that currently covers the lake would be exposed and could be put into cultivation. The fertile volcanic soils of the surrounding countries have had to create very rich lake sediments. The rains in most of it are enough for a good harvest.

With the simple emptying of the great lake, a harvest could be obtained in 7 million hectares. This extension is sufficient to produce food for all five East African States, deficits in this area.

By channelling the waters of the rivers that currently form the lake, a second crop could be obtained during the dry season, or the cultivation without interruption. This would create an intensely cultivated agricultural nucleus, similar to Egypt.

In addition, this lake has the advantage that its submerged lands belong to several bordering States: Tanzania, Uganda and Kenya, which have the greatest food problems and a disproportionate population.

Territory, population and considerations:

The real drawback of the project on Lake Victoria is the climatic modification that could cause the plateaus. The air recharges moisture upon reaching the lake and causes considerable rainfall in the surrounding mountains. Now this is nothing more than a completely unconfirmed theory. It would be necessary to know to what extent the same rains would occur or less in the mountains of Rwanda, Uganda and Kenya if the lake did not exist. In the high mountains it would rain anyway in great abundance, the evaporation that occurs in Lake Victoria is not the cause of its rains.

The lake, 70,000 km2, has huge evaporation losses. If we make the comparison between the amount of total rainfall that falls on the surrounding territory and the amount of water that evaporates from Lake Victoria, we will see that there is a huge disproportion. Roughly we can say that from Lake Victoria, according to calculations made long ago, about 2,000 m3 / s evaporate, but the rains that come from around represent a significantly higher figure.

Now, where it could have a notable effect is on the plain of Uganda itself, north of the lake. However, the southern half of the lake is quite arid, so it is not seen that the lake has so much climatic influence, no matter how much the winds usually blow from the east and midday. But this is not completely true. If we analyse the question carefully, we will see that the influence on the local climate of the lake is quite small. In the plains of Uganda, it rains more because they are within the equatorial convection line and it is partly Congolese winds that humidify them. We must clarify all the details and reach certain conclusions.

Let's not cause a climate disaster. In principle, I do not think so, dog it is necessary to check.

And if such a thing did not happen, then the project would be free, because this is one of the simplest devices offered by terrestrial geography. The lake, at 1.1.30 ms above the sea, can be emptied with extreme ease. River flooding works, partly from volcanic territories, must have left a very fertile ground. The desiccation of the lake would mean the cultivation of a territory of 7 million hectares that, grown for rice, for example, could produce 30 million tons, and cultivated corn, 20 million. A barn for extremely poor countries.

In addition, this lake has the advantage that its submerged lands belong to several bordering States: Tanzania, Uganda and Kenya, which have the greatest food problems and a disproportionate population.

PROPOSAL:

"December 1984

Dear Mr. President.

I am pleased to address you, as President of the Organization for African Unity, to submit for the consideration of that International Organization a proposal concerning the use of the agrarian possibilities of Lake Victoria, which I will briefly discuss.

As is known, Lake Ukerewe or Victoria is a vast reservoir of water, 7 million hectares and a maximum depth of 80 meters, at 1,135 meters above sea level. Actually, it is a large, very shallow swamp, which covers a very large territory, whose bottom has to be fertile.

The proposal we have allowed ourselves to make is the following. Due to its altitude and the rapid descent that follows, the Nile Victoria could easily be emptied, deepening the Nile channel a few tens of meters. Thus, almost all the surface that currently covers the lake would be exposed and could be put into cultivation. The fertile volcanic soils of the surrounding countries have had to create very rich lake sediments. The rains in most of it are enough for a good harvest. With the simple emptying of the great lake, a harvest could be obtained in 7 million hectares. This extension is sufficient to produce food for all five East African States, deficits in this area.

By channelling the waters of the rivers that currently form the lake, a second crop could be obtained during the dry season, or the cultivation without interruption. This would create an intensely cultivated agricultural nucleus, similar to Egypt.

In addition, the lake is a vast evaporation field, which causes the Nile to lose much of the water it should carry. Indeed, it comes out of it with a flow of 600 m3 when it should carry at least 1,500 m3 / second. This would increase the irrigation capacity of the Nile at the bottom of its course, which would be a considerable benefit for this part of the World.

The only drawback that we find is that the lake helps recharge the clouds that rain over the surrounding mountains, which may lead to climate change, which we cannot measure well, but which would surely be less than we think. This is the drawback, which would be far exceeded by the advantage of having 7 million hectares of fertile land, which could accommodate most of the population of East African countries.

If the territory currently covered by the lake were planted with rice, for example, at 4 tons per hectare, the production could be 30 million tons. If corn were planted, 20 million tons. With this, Tanzania and the rest of the countries surrounding the lake would have sufficient food resources. The emptying operation is technically simple, and the cultivation of the emerged fund could be carried out with great ease. It would only be to win a large agricultural space now wasted.

From far away Europe the Ukerewe is a legendary lake, mythical. But the need to ensure the survival of man removes all sentimentality from us. If this project is feasible, it is the food base on which the surrounding States can be solidly supported.

I express the most vivid expressions of respect and solidarity and send you my best regards.

Juan Sanz Sanz"

Drainage and cultivation of the Tabasco Plains

1984

SYNOPSIS:

This coastal strip is the most extensive alluvial territory that Mexico has, with a length on the coast of 600 or 700 kilometres and a width that varies from 50 to 150 kilometres. The total extension is 5 to 6 million hectares.

But the great rains that fall on the region, plus the flooding of rivers from other territories that reach it, make it an agriculturally very poor territory, with great hardship use.

However, in my modest opinion, Mexico has here its best chance of solving the food problems that afflict it. This territory, if cultivated exclusively of rice, could yield a crop of 20 to 30 million tons. Is this a sufficient reason to attempt its use.

<u>Territory and considerations</u>

Mexico.

Here we find abundant fertile soil and water together, with an excess of water to be controlled; The Mexican alluvial plain has about 5 million hectares.

There is a coastal plain between Veracruz and Cozumel, about 1,200 kilometres in length, and an average depth of 100 km. Thus, we have a fertile territory to take advantage of 120,000 square kilometres, 12 Mha, which could reach 15 with a better use of the Yucatan.

Mexico has major food problems, a population of almost 80 million people (* 1984), a really delicate situation. And that, at the doors of the USA. UU.

We see, then, that there is arable land and that there is the same problem here as in Asita Tropical, where the great rains flood the low, alluvial lands, cover them with jungles and swamps.

Floods make agriculture impossible. You cannot get even most of these lowland and alluvial lands at least once a year. Two, much less.

Here, as already said, the same device can be applied as in Tropical Asia:

First, contain the rivers, to prevent flooding, on the one hand, and to retain water for the dry season.

Second, leave the lower channels to serve as a drain to the rains of the lower regions.

Third, distribute the waters along the low Plain in the dry season.

The Usumacinta is the largest river in the area. The basin has 102,000 square kilometres. With average rains of 1,500 in the middle and high valley, although its flow is relatively modest from 1,000 to 1,500 m3.

According to Vidal de la Blanche, it has been possible to establish the runoff of Mexican rivers, which is as follows:

Pacific slope, 84,000 Mm3 / year, 2,600 m3 / s., 70%

Atlantic slope, 210.520 Mm3 / year, 6.700 m3 / s., 28%

Indoor, 6,500 Mm3 / year, 180 m3 / s., 2%

In the coastal plains of the tropical zone the soils are of good quality, deep, virgin, largely covered with forests and chaparral in less humid areas.

The Yucatan Peninsula almost lacks soil, so agriculture is barely practiced.

The coastal region needs drainage for its use. Also, the coastal floods of the extra tropical region are deep and fertile; Here irrigation is essential.

The Papaloapan River flows about 50 kilometres SE of Veracruz; It has a length of 420 kilometres. Next to the mouth is the San Juan, 210 km. This last river crosses the plain between the San Martin de Tuxla mountain range and the plateau. The Papaloapan has an intramontane valley between the Sierra de los Mixtecas and the Madre de Oaxaca.

The rains fall abundantly in the latter (2 to 3 ms), while in the valley of Tehuacán we find an arid region, with rains that fall to 400l.

In the Yucatan it rains from May to October, between 1 to 2 ms.

In the first place, it rains enough in these plains so that a crop is possible during the rainy season, in summer. The problem is the abundant jungle, which should be deforested, and the excess water overflowed in the lower part. So the first task would be to cultivate the low plain for the rainy season. This requires three things:

First. Replace the forest with crop fields.

Second. Give way to the waters of the swamps.

Third. Retain river flooding.

The alluvial region of the Gulf plains, are divided into two sections, separated by the Tuxla mountain range: one in Veracruz and one in Tabasco-Campeche. The first one is 200 km in front of the coast and 50-60 deep: an area of 10,000 km2, 1 Mhas. The second is larger, with a front of 300 km and an average depth of 100; that is, 30,000 km2, 3 million hectares. Together, this double low plain, alluvial, has about 4 million hectares fully usable.

For 30,000 km2 and taking into account that a first harvest would be carried out due to the abundant rains in the region, with 1,000 m3 / s is sufficient, which ensures an irrigation of 1 m3 / m3. It is clear that, with the water of Usumacinta, Grijalva, etc., it is enough, because it is not about cultivating an arid territory and watering twice a year, but only once, since the other does the rains.

The most complex problem is in Yucatan, where it is said that there is no soil, so agriculture is not practiced. But there is lush vegetation, where rains are abundant. Therefore, there is a breakdown of surface limestones, which allow the existence of the jungle.

PROPOSAL:

"December 1984.

Dear Sir:

I am pleased to address you. To submit to the Government of the United States of Mexico a proposal or suggestion concerning the agricultural use of the alluvial territories of the southern coast of the Gulf of Mexico, which in summary consists of the following:

This coastal strip is the most extensive alluvial territory that Mexico has, with a length on the coast of 600 or 700 kilometres and a width that varies from 50 to 150 kilometres. The total extension is 5 to 6 million hectares.

But the great rains that fall on the region, plus the flooding of rivers from other territories that reach it, make it an agriculturally very poor territory, with great hardship use.

However, in my modest opinion, Mexico has here its best chance of solving the food problems that afflict it. This territory, if cultivated exclusively of rice, could yield a crop of 20 to 30 million tons. Is this a sufficient reason to attempt its use.

For this reason, the proposal that I allow myself to propose consists in facilitating the exit of the waters, expanding and deepening the river channels now existing, and retaining the avenues of the foreign rivers at the exit of the mountains. This would result in flooding and leaving most of the land free of floods, which would be ready for cultivation.

It is a considerable work - but technically feasible - and the results that would be obtained from its execution would be of invaluable value to the vigorous Mexican State, which needs a very firm agrarian base with which to meet the growing food needs of a superabundant population and whose industrial development cannot be locked by the requirement to cover, in part, that deficit through third countries.

In addition, the great local rains would allow to obtain a harvest during the summertime and the retention of the waters of the other rivers during the dry season, and even the cultivation of constant form.

In the hope that the ideas presented may be useful, I send a cordial greeting.

Juan Sanz Sanz"

White Nile

1983

SYNOPSIS:

Africa is an ancient continent, of hard lands, in which good lands are scarce. There are few deep alluvial spaces. The oldest is in the bucket of Chad. There is another one in the middle Niger and this one from the Bahr el Gazal-White Nile, which should have an extension of perhaps 100,000 km2, approximately the space that the swamps occupy today. These good lands have an invaluable value. As here the rains are between 500 and 1,000 litters, with a rainy season and a dry season, rain crops could be established, in dry land.

This would be an invaluable help for the Republic of the Sudan, an overpopulated country with low food capacity. At present this region of floods is uninhabited, which would facilitate its colonization.

If these swamps could really be drained by the procedure of deepening the bed of the White Nile below them, the consequences that this would report would be really remarkable.

But the most notable advantage that the desiccation of the swamps would produce would be the recovery of the waters that are lost in them. This volume of water, which we have calculated at 2,000 m3 / s would double the flow of the Nile in the lower course. With this, the capacity of irrigation and hydroelectric production would also double.

PROJECT:

INTEGRAL USE OF WHITE NILE WATERS AND ITS REPERCUSSIONS IN THE COUNTRIES OF THE AREA.

One.

As is known, the Nile is formed by two large branches, which meet in Khartoum: The Blue Nile, from the mountains of Ethiopia, and the White Nile, from the mountains of Rwanda. Seen as a whole, the Nile is one of the largest rivers in the world because of its length and the length of its basin, but not because of its flow, which in Egypt barely reaches 2,000 m3 / second; that is, more or less like Rhin. As the Nile crosses the Sahara in the lower half of its course; It could be believed that the cause of its low flow in relation to its basin is due to the fact that it is a river that runs through desert countries, with little rain. However, it is not so; It rains heavily in the southern half of its basin - in the Ethiopian mountains, in southern Sudan, in the Great Lakes region. There are abundant monsoon rains in Tropical Africa along the Nile. Its flow should be several times what it becomes, and this requires an explanation.

On the other hand, almost all the waters of the Nile in Egypt come from the Blue Nile. The floodwaters of this river are enormous, reaching 7,500 m3 / s in September, while in the winter and spring months it hardly carries water. The Blue Nile is the one who maintained the fertilization and drought flood oscillations during which it was cultivated that was the main feature of Egypt until the construction of the Assuan Dam. The White Nile, which has a fairly modest swell in summer, maintains a relatively regular flow during the outflow, which partly compensates for the large Blue Nile runoff.

But we stumble upon the surprising fact that the White Nile, which brings to Egypt only one third of the water that reaches there, is a much longer river, with a larger basin and rainier than the Blue. At the confluence of Khartoum, the Ethiopian arm provides 7,500 m3 / s of flood and 180 in waste, while the arm that comes from Lake Victoria has 1,040 m3 / s in flood and 380 m3 / s in waste. The White Nile has a length of more than 3,000 km, between the mountains of Rwanda and Khartoum; its basin is one million km2 long and in most of it it rains a lot. In the mountains where it has its sources the rains are exceptional in some places. Here you have enough power to create and sustain the huge Victoria Lake, whose water has to be constantly renewed because of evaporation losses. It leaves this lake with a flow of 600 m3 / s. Upon reaching the marshes of southern Sudan, its flow has doubled. These marshes receive the waters of the White Nile, but also those of the Bahr el Gazal basin, which is fed by abundant rains in the mountains bordering the Congo.

And this is where the phenomenon that is the key to our project occurs.

Two.

The southern Sudan forms a vast flat basin, with very little slope, whose only exit is the White Nile in the direction of Khartoum. It is an alluvial plain, covered with swamps, in which the waters that reach it stop, stagnate and evaporate for the most part. This is the reason why the Great Lakes Nile enters the swamps with a flow of more than 1,000 m3 / s and leaves with much less. But to the flow of the Nile it is necessary to add the waters that fall into the basin itself, especially those that come from the mountains that separate it from the Congo basin.

These swamps cover an area of around 100,000 km2 and are fed by this set of rivers.

In tropical countries the phenomenon of evaporation acts with extreme power, causing any aquatic surface to lose between one and a half meters and more than two meters a year. In all the enormous extension of the swamps, about two meters of water is lost by evaporation in the whole of the year, producing oscillations in the extension and depth of the marshes. In spite of this, there is a rest of evergreen swamps. Through fairly simple calculations, it is concluded that the White Nile and its tributaries in the Bahr el Gazal basin lose a flow equivalent to more than 2,000 m3 / second - which is as much as the Nile has in Egypt - and leaves them with a known flow in Khartoum: 1-040 m3 in flood and 380 in wastewater. But the White Nile flood waters they do not come, in fact, from the swamps, but from Sobat, an atypical river like the Blue Nile, which joins the White Nile just at the point where the swamps end and it begins its solitary course in the direction of the Sudanese capital.

For this reason, the White Nile itself, which is nothing more than a swamp drain, draws a fairly low flow from these, which should be approximately its discharge flow: 380 m3 / s. It is a ridiculous amount in relation to the rains received by its basin and that expresses the magnitude of the evaporation that occurs in the marshes above. Here they lose between 2,000 and 3,000 m3 / s. And this water flow is what human ingenuity should try to rescue.

Three.

Throughout history, the marshes of the Bahr el Gazal have been a formidable obstacle for travellers: a horizontal plain, covered with papyrus and ambach, without defined courses, more than 500 km long and in which it was not possible stocking up, it kept unknown sources of the Nile until last century. Being within the area of irradiation of the oldest culture, the countries located on the other side of the swamps remained strangers to it. A little over a century ago, Europeans definitively discovered the sources of the Nile, but not going up the river, but reaching the Great Lakes from the east coast and then down it. So we are faced with a physical fact that has had negligible repercussions in history. Worse, in turn, the great swamp deprives Egypt of half of its water, since very little of what it contains reaches it.

Four.

The desiccation of these swamps is, at first sight, a very difficult problem. The slope is very small and it is difficult to run the water without stagnating. The average sea level of this water plain is 450 meters. Khartoum is 388 meters away. There is an unevenness of approximately 70 meters. In the vicinity of Malakal, the swamps end, and the waters of the Nile, Bahr el Gazal and Sobat meet. From here the White Nile no longer receives perennial tributaries. To ensure that the waters of this region do not get bogged down, it would be necessary to take advantage of the slope that exists below, deepening the river courses and placing the bottom of the beds at a lower point several meters. In turn, these should be expanded, to receive water flows greater than today.

The bottom of the basin are deep floods, which occupy a large area and accompany the course of the Nile from its exit from the mountains of Uganda to approximately the point where the river that connects the capital with the southern provinces cuts the river. It is precisely this subsoil of floods that motivates the extreme horizontality of the plain. Even so, there is an unevenness that could be exploited. To the north of alluvial subsoil, in the direction of Khartoum, the river begins the crossing of hard bottoms, generally sandstones, through which it makes its way laboriously. If we take the Khartoum altitude as a reference point for the reduction of the riverbed level, it would be in the stretch of hard bottoms between the railway line and Khartoum where a really difficult and expensive job would be done. In the section on alluvial funds the work it would be much simpler, a kind of dredging.

It is not my purpose to go into details about matters in which I am not a specialist, but merely an amateur. These conclusions follow from the simple observation of the maps and, perhaps, seen the problems in more detail, the conclusions will be entirely opposite. What does seem obvious is that, deepening the bed of the White Nile between Malakal and Khartoum, the swamps would be emptied, the riverbeds above, on alluvial terrain, would take shape, and the waters that would come from subsequent rains would not stagnate. already. With this, the double advantage would be obtained of preventing the marshes from being the vast evaporation field they are today, causing the rivers that reach them to reach almost all their flow, and, at the same time, an alluvial terrain would be exposed. deep and rich, it could be cultivated. The mere possibility that this is so is reason enough to find out to what extent it is true.

In recent geological times the marshes had an exit and were captured by a tributary of the Blue Nile, forming the swamp drain that is now the White Nile. In this way the human industry would only finish the work that the river has been doing for thousands of years.

Five.

If these swamps could really be drained by the procedure of deepening the bed of the White Nile below them, the consequences that this would report would be really remarkable.

Africa is an ancient continent, of hard lands, in which good lands are scarce. There are few deep alluvial spaces. The oldest is in the bucket of Chad. There is another one in the middle Niger and this one from the Bahr el Gazal-White Nile, which should have an extension of perhaps 100,000 km2, approximately the space that the swamps occupy today. These good lands have an invaluable value. As here the rains are between 500 and 1,000 litters, with a rainy season and a dry season, rain crops could be established, in dry land. This would be an invaluable help for the Republic of the Sudan, an overpopulated country with low food capacity. At present this region of floods is uninhabited, which would facilitate its colonization.

Six.

But the most notable advantage that the desiccation of the swamps would produce would be the recovery of the waters that are lost in them. This volume of water, which we have calculated at 2,000 m3 / s would double the flow of the Nile in the lower course. With this, the capacity of irrigation and hydroelectric production would also double In the huge Assuan reservoir, evaporation causes the loss of several hundred cubic meters per second of water. With this, the Nile's irrigation capacity in Egypt is greatly diminished. However, it was inevitable to build such a large pond because Egypt needed energy to electrify and in those times, it could only be taken out of the river. For this, the dam had to be raised more than 100 meters, motivating a really excessive water pond. Water that came from the White Nile would not suffer this handicap. Possibly more than double the energy capacity of the hydroelectric station.

In turn, the risks of Egypt and those of the Blue Nile, together with Khartoum, could be considerably expanded, increasing food capacity and the production of agricultural raw materials for industry. Perhaps that dilemma that so many overpopulated countries have between using their arable land to produce food or using it to obtain agricultural materials for commercial purposes is over. Perhaps these countries, with larger irrigated areas, would not see how their cotton or orange crops, which they need to obtain dividends, prevented the production of food that the population needs to survive.

Egypt is a case of extreme overpopulation. The narrowness of the valley through which the Nile runs prevents that in most of the course the risks could be extended. These new irrigations would not necessarily have to be established on alluvial lands such as riverside rivers. Water works miracles, even in areas that are less fertile in appearance, and artificial fertilizers can do the rest. The extension of the irrigation could be carried out in the coastal region, on both sides of the delta, extending westward, since from El Alamein the coast is cliffed by depressions, below sea level, which is south of Marmorica, in the direction of the Libyan border. Although the bottom of these depressions is muddy and brackish, perhaps they could be cultivated with some previous work.

Seven.

As the irrigation capacity of the new waters of the White Nile will possibly exceed the extent of the land that could be effectively cultivated in Egypt and Sudan, we will find in that case a surplus of water that could be used for a purpose of great importance today: lay a solid material basis for the pacification of the countries of the Middle East (* 1983).

Indeed, among the many problems that these countries have, perhaps the most serious and profound is the lack of water.

Without water they cannot produce food, nor can industries work or urban agglomerations exist. If this base is lacking, everything else cannot give fullness. The lack of water causes a precarious situation in those societies that make them vulnerable to all kinds of conflicts. They are like a weak body - dehydrated - in which calamities are primed. The excess Nilotic water could well serve to remedy its evil. All these countries produce less food than they need, and the development of their industries is limited by the lack of water. Lacking those States of a firm base, they are easy prey to the interests of third countries, toys in the hands of those who help them to sustain themselves, since they themselves are not capable. All these countries depend on foreign aid; They do not suffice themselves. Without this outside help, they would soon enter a dramatic situation.

This support is very expensive for those who maintain it and, although from the political point of view it does not cease to have its advantages for them, there is no doubt that what it costs to the USA, the USSR and the Arab oil countries is such an exorbitant amount to year, that the execution of this project would be a relief, in case it is really feasible; that is to say, that great water flow can be recovered from the marshes of the South Sudan.

Eight.

A large irrigation canal could derive from the Nile in the vicinity of Cairo, cross the Sinai desert, reach the Philistine coast and through the depression of the Yezreel, penetrate the Ghor, the Jordan valley, irrigating it. The water of this river was diverted to the coast by the Israelites and this is one of the great reasons for conflict. Now the Palestinian coast and depression could be irrigated, involving the project to Israel and Jordan. On the other hand, water could be used not only by gravity - that is, by pouring it below the flow rate - but by elevation, since in the Mediterranean countries the elevation of 100 or 200 meters of water is not burdensome. This could also fertilize the southern part of Lebanon. If the water could reach Syria in abundance, the solution will be round, although this country does not have that problem, since the Euphrates and the Orontes give it a drink.

Nine.

On the other hand, if the expansion of the Egyptian irrigation was made by the depressions to the West of the Delta, and thus reaching the Libyan border, we would have the basis to solve another problem. Libya is possibly the thirstiest country. Without permanent rivers, with regular rains only in a small part of the territory, it suffers a really pronounced water deficit, which is to alleviate with increasingly deep perforations or water treatment plants that produce water at the price of gold. But Libya not only needs water to drink and cultivate, but for the development of its petrochemical industry. As long as it does not have enough water, Libya will not be able to equip itself with a petrochemical industry and thus take full advantage of the resources of its deposits, as Algeria and Venezuela have done. This country, with considerable financial capacity, could be a very interested part in the execution of this project, which would allow it to take a great step forward. In turn, this water received by Libya from Egypt would be a stabilizing factor, by creating an interdependence between the two States, so that the potential reasons for a conflict would diminish.

Ten.

Finally, we stumble upon the most acute problem of how many occur today in this part of the world: the Palestinian problem (* 1983). In large part it has its origin in the dispute over land and water. The Palestinians have been dispossessed in large numbers of their lands and have been forced to emigrate, either to other Palestinian territories, where they form very dense agglomerations, well abroad. If, by bringing water for the irrigation of large areas of Israel and Jordan, a general improvement was achieved, the Palestinians - refugees or not - would also benefit from it. This would end an anomalous, dramatic situation, which in turn is the kiss for new conflicts to arise periodically. There would be room for everyone. Thus, in Palestine we attend a bitter dispute over a place under the sun, in which the one who is momentarily stronger.

We are convinced that the interdependence created between the countries of this area for the common use of the remaining waters of the Nile - in the case, I repeat, that this project is really feasible - would be a powerful stabilization factor. We believe that Muslim and Hebrew societies are not antagonistic; They have coexisted for many centuries and can continue to do so. It is necessary, for this, to solve the underlying problems, that there are no situations in which the survival of one depends on the annihilation of the other. It is necessary to find balance, stability.

Eleven.

Finally, the possibilities of exploitation of the Nile do not end here. This is only the first phase, from the recoverable waters of the swamps of South Sudan, a project that I can only offer in theory and whose reality will be the specialists who determine.

If the marshes of the Bahr el Gazal are a vast evaporation field, whose correction we have already seen the consequences that would be reported, Lake Victoria, with its almost 70,000 km2, is not less, in which a flow of water is lost for the same cause water that is not less than 2,000 m3 / s that can surely be obtained from the marshes. For this, it is necessary to carry out a work that, at first glance, seems inconceivable: the drying up of the great lake. With this, two things would be obtained, as in the Bahr el Gazal, a large area of arable land at the bottom of the lake and a very remarkable water flow that, along with the one obtained below, would triple the current flow of the Nile. Lake Victoria is shallow and high altitude. To empty it, it would be enough to deepen the Nile that serves as a drain in 30 or 40 meters.

There may be a slight change in the climate, but the benefit of having such a large area of land, around which are countries with such severe overpopulation problems as Uganda, Burundi, Rwanda, Kenya and Tanzania, counteracts any objection. What some years ago seemed inconceivable, today may be necessary and tomorrow inevitable.

PROPOSAL:

"April 1983.

Mr President.

I am pleased to address you to submit to the North-South Commission for consideration an idea that, at first glance, seems interesting: the integral hydraulic exploitation of the Nile, which is now only used in about half of it. Indeed, the waters of the White Nile get bogged down and evaporate mostly in the marshes of the Bahr el Gazal. If these waters, which surely have almost as much volume as those that run through Khartoum to the sea, were not lost by evaporation, but had an outlet and could be used for irrigation and, in addition, the enormous alluvial space was earned for cultivation which today cover, the economic consequences for the countries of the area would not be negligible.

With the desire that what is exposed in the project fits reality, receive a cordial greeting.

Juan Sanz Sanz"

Congo River

and

Lake Tchad

1986 y 1987

SYNOPSIS:

So that the waters of the Congo River fertilize the plains located to the North, I propose the following works:

Retention of the waters of the Congo River immediately above Kinshasa, by means of a 70 meters high dike, which would create an artificial lake of more than 300,000 square kilometres in length, raising the level of the waters to the city of Bangui.

Opening a gap through the Acrocoro de Asande.

Water distribution across the plains of the Sahel.

And, the proposal we make for Chad, consists of shaping and deepening the old Bahr el Gazal drain, so that the flood waters are deposited in the Bodele Depression, rather than in Lake Tchad.

PROJETCS:

IDEAS FOR A WATER DEVIATION PROJECT OF THE CONGO RIVER TOWARDS THE PLAINS SAHELIANAS.

I will be allowed to present some elementary facts, well known but necessary:

1 The Congo River is a sterile giant. With a flow of more than 40,000 m3 / second, the second the world, it hardly serves anything.

Isolated from the sea, interrupted its course and that of its tributaries by several waterfall lines, it crosses very unhealthy jungle and swampy regions.

2 The plains of the Sahel, on the edge of the desert, suffer, not only lack of abundant rains, but extreme climatic irregularity. But there are huge extensions of arable land in them.

The proposal that I am pleased to make is basically the conjunction of two complementary elements: the Congo basin and the Sahelian plains. In the first the water is left over and in the second it is missing. The first is almost sterile from an agricultural point of view and the second has huge areas of arable land. So that the waters of the Congo River fertilize the plains located to the North, I propose the following works:

First: Retention of the waters of the Congo River immediately above Kinshasa, by means of a 70-meter high dike, which would create an artificial lake of more than 300,000 square kilometres in length, raising the water level to the city of Bangui.

Second: Opening a gap through the Acrocoro de Asande, which separates the Congo and Chari basins, using the explosives of extraordinary power that currently exist and other ultramodern techniques.

Third: Distribution of the waters along the plains of the Sahel, basically as follows: a) Take advantage of the natural slope of the Chari-Lake Chad-Bodele River Depression system, to irrigate most of the Chad's basin, to the limits of Tibesti (here would be the main crop core). b) As the exit of the waters of the Congo to the northern slope would be at an altitude above the sea of 350 meters, the same as that of Bangui, a part of them, by means of a channel that maintained said altitude, could go towards the West through Northern Nigeria, bordering the North and the Niger Arch, etc. c) Deviation of a part of the waters of the Congo to the Benué river, navigable river, which would allow access from the sea to the great Congo lake.

The consequences could be the following:

The flow of the Congo River is 43,000 cubic meters / second. As much water as necessary can be extracted from it, enough to irrigate the desired extensions to the north, in the Tchad basin.

The hydroelectric station next to Kinshasa would give this country as much energy as it could need in a long time.

The large central lake would be connected by the sea through the canals and the lower Benue-Niger river. The interior of the Congo would cease to be completely isolated, both the Republic of Zaire now swampy and almost uninhabited in the territory that would occupy the lake, as the Central African Republic.

The irrigation and navigation channel towards the Niger Arch would allow a series of irrigated spaces to be created in the territories of Cameroon, Nigeria, Niger, Mali, Mauritania, which would definitely solve the problem of hunger in this part of the world.

<u>**The difficulties are as follows:**</u>

Colossal work would require huge investments, which interested countries are far from being able to make.

The Republic of Zaire would see a space of 350,000 square kilometres flooded, approximately one seventh of its total area. But it is a space that, because of the enormous power of the river, is now very unhelpful. On the contrary, it would gain a great source of energy and, above all, an inland navigation space, equivalent to the Great Lakes of North America, communicated, like these, with the sea.

PROPOSAL

USE OF THE HYDRAULIC SYSTEM OF LAKE TCHAD.

"November 1986.

Dear Mr. Minister:

I am pleased to address you, to submit a proposal or suggestion for the use of the hydraulic and agricultural resources of the Lake Tchad system for the consideration of your Government. Vividly impressed by the enormous effort that France is making to reach a stable and lasting solution for the troubled Central African country, and aware that this will not be possible as long as there is no firm material base, I have allowed myself to suggest this possibility, which happened to briefly expose

As is known, the waters of a vast river network are deposited in

Lake Tchad, whose main courses are Chari, Logone and Komadugu. This lake is nothing but the result of a great summer flood, which also covers vast territories in the middle course of the rivers. But Lake Tchad does not occupy the lowest point of the depression, but it is located in the Bodele, 300 kilometres to the Northeast. In rainier times than today, the waters of Lake Tchad poured into the Bodelé through the course, today dry, of the Bahr el Gazal. The Tchad is a simple swamp, of variable extension, with a maximum depth of less than 10 meters and at a height above sea level of approximately 280 meters. On the contrary, the Bodele Depression has a vast extension below 200 meters above sea level. Therefore, the waters of Tchad could easily be decanted towards the Bodele.

The proposal we make consists of shaping and deepening

the old Bahr el Gazal drain, so that the floodwaters are definitively deposited in the Bodele Depression, rather than in Lake Tchad.

By deepening river channels and exiting the waters, swampy lands would be free of flooding and could be put into cultivation. First, the extent that Lake Chad currently covers. By having a lower point, flood waters would no longer stagnate, but could be used for irrigation where necessary.

With this simple drainage operation, a large alluvial space would be earned for cultivation. The waters diverted to the Bodele could give rise to a second irrigated region, since only part of the depression would be occupied by the definitive pond of rains throughout the basin. Thus, a first harvest would be obtained during the summer seasons. In a second phase, retaining the waters of the summer rains in the high courses of the rivers, a second harvest would be achieved during the dry season and even the cultivation without interruption. The whole of the depression is formed by alluvial soils, so that its agricultural use is feasible. Only the water is missing. That is to say, the water is left over at this time and the land it covers must be left uncovered, to subsequently channel this same water to the flood-free territories.

This is, in summary, the proposal that I have allowed myself to address to the Government of France, a party that is extremely interested in resolving this conflict, certain that, if feasible, the active and admirable French policy and its considerable economic power will be able to take advantage.

Yours sincerely,

Juan Sanz Sanz"

"July 1987.

Dear Sir:

I am pleased to send you the brief attached study, "Ideas for a project to divert the waters of the Congo River to the Sahelian plains", in which I present some hypothetical solutions to the problems of Sub-Saharan Africa, it is about harnessing the enormous power of the Congo River, a sterile giant, which may be the driving force that sets the African continent in motion, solving with its waters the most serious of its problems: the scarcity of food resources, a base without which society cannot progress.

And I address you and the Government of France, first, because it is a possibility whose execution would require the collective effort of the international community; and, secondly, because the admirable commitment of France, through the Ministry that you lead, is known by all to benefit these countries as much as possible.

That is why I appeal to your Government to take into consideration the possibility suggested here, although its realization is extremely expensive and very long term.

Yours sincerely,

Juan Sanz Sanz"

River network
of the
River Plata
1987

SYNOPSIS:

The proposal consists of remove from the main plain the mass of water of the Parana, pouring it in the course of the Uruguay river by its retention at the height of Posadas and its channelling through a channel to the alveus of the Uruguay river, 100 kilometres away.

The channel of the Uruguay River is more defined than that of the Parana and its distance to the lower much smaller. The first issue on which we are not sure is Uruguay's channel is capable of admitting its current flow of 8,000 metrs3 / second, plus 18,000 meters3 / second of Parana, that is, a water mass of 26,000 meters3 / second in the mouth.

If that were the case, that is, if the waters of the two great rivers could flow through the riverbed of Uruguay, the consequences would be very noticeable on the region that is currently being flooded. in it from Posadas, particularly those of the Paraguay River. In this way they would circulate through the riverbed less leaving the main bed (several tens of kilometres) free for cultivation. In the dry season, that is, when these tributaries are not enough to maintain the minimum level, Parana Superior itself could provide the necessary water to maintain the level that allows the work of the river ports along the great river.

PROJECT:

IDEAS FOR A PROJECT OF REGULATION OF THE RIVERS OF THE FLUVIAL DEL PLATA NETWORK.

I will be allowed to present some general facts, well known, but no less necessary.

The Río de la Plata is the third river current on Earth, after the Amazon and the Congo, with an approximate flow at the mouth of 35,000 m3 / second. Of the three great rivers that form it, Uruguay, Paraguay and Parana, it is the latter, by far, the most powerful. Formed the Parana in Brazilian territory, it crosses extremely rainy regions and its flow in the streams of Sete Quedas is 14,000 m3 / second and at the entrance into Argentine territory it will not be less than 18,000 m3 / second. Just the Iguazu River It has

1,750, leading to the waterfalls and the border.

The great floods are not caused only by the action of the waters of the Parana on the plain. They occur when the floodwaters are added to those of the remaining rivers, especially those of Paraguay. But it is true that the main body of water involved is that of Paraná. Therefore, although it is not the only cause, it is the main cause and we must act on it.

At the height of Posadas, the Paran drags a flow of approximately 18,000 m3 / second. Although the floods in the Argentine plains are due both to the action of the rivers and to the lack of spontaneous drainage of many regions, it is undoubted that the main cause of them is the spill of such a huge body of water as the one that the Parana drags.

When these factors converge - lack of spontaneous drainage and flooding of large rivers. Catastrophic floods occur. These have been repeated tenaciously in recent years.

The proposal consists of separating the water mass of the Paraná from the main plain, pouring it into the course of the Uruguay River by its retention at the height of Posadas and its channelling through a channel to the alveus of the Uruguay River, 100 kilometres away.

The channel of the Uruguay River is more defined than that of the Parana and its distance to the lower riverbed mouth. The first issue on which we are not sure is Uruguay's channel is capable of admitting its current flow of 8,000 metrs3 / second, plus 18,000 meters3 / second of Parana, that is, a water mass of 26,000 meters3 / second in the mouth

If that were the case, that is, if the waters of the two great rivers could flow through the riverbed of Uruguay, the consequences would be very noticeable on the region that is currently being flooded. The Argentine Parana riverbed would only receive the waters that flow in it from Posadas, particularly those of the Paraguay River. In this way they would circulate through the riverbed less leaving the main bed (several tens of kilometres) free for cultivation. In the dry season, that is, when these tributaries are not enough to maintain the minimum level, High Parana itself could provide the necessary water to maintain the level that allows the work of the river ports along the great river.

The Parana River is a giant that must be tamed; His strength must be useful to men and not a constant calamity. Through the simple operation - although expensive - of diverting its course, perhaps that result could be obtained.

The greater bed of the Parana river in Argentine territory,

independently of the Pampas plains, has an extension of 150,000 square kilometres, it seems.

t is the territory where floods are mainly primed and, for this reason, must be abandoned to the vagaries of the river. If a relatively constant flow flow through the Parana, especially based on the waters of the Paraguay River, they would cross exclusively the smaller river bed and the rest of the bed that the Paraná has excavated in the general plain, very fertile as a whole, it could be intensively taken advantage of, with the advantage of having water for its cultivation of the rains during the season of these and of the irrigation during the drought. That is, a territory of constant, uninterrupted cultivation, capable of producing huge amounts of food.

By lowering the level of the waters in the main riverbeds, their general reduction would take place and both the tributary rivers and the flooded plains would have a better spontaneous drainage, so that the effect of the marginal flood would be much lower and it would be easier to attempt to the surrounding regions artificial drainage. The key is in the separation of the general plain of the waters of the Brazilian Parana.

As for the excess of water that would circulate through the channel of Uruguay, there is no doubt that it would be detrimental for that country in a first stage. But we must bear in mind that the river would then become navigable and link to the upper part of Paraná. It would be, then, a formidable way of navigation, in a territory that now lacks it. Trade, in part, would lean toward him. On the other hand, the hydroelectric station of Posadas, from the waters of the Paraná let run by its current bed to compensate for the sewage, could supply to that country good part of the energy that needs.

Such is the proposal that I am pleased to propose to the government of the Argentine Republic.

Finally, I would not want to succinctly expose another possibility, about the use of the Paraguay River. As is known, this river is born in the Mato Grosso and forms a swampy region where it loses a good part of its waters. The Pantanal del Alto Paraguay is the result of the lack of exit of the river due to archaic outcrops in the region that crosses the railroad from Sao Paulo to La Paz. Deepening the riverbed at that point, the exit of the waters would be facilitated and with that the ones that evaporate in the plain would be recovered, at the same time that it would be arable, being free from flooding. Once the waters of Alto Paraguay are liberated, its flow would increase considerably. The reclaimed waters, instead of flowing through the channel of Paraguay to Parana, could be totally or partially diverted with a channel that follows approximately 100 meters above the sea, obliquely towards the interior of the Chaco, irrigating an enormous territory of the western margin of Paraguay from the Argentine-Brazilian border to the Mountain Range of Cordoba. Irrigated territory could also generate huge agricultural productions.

SUGGESTING:

"March 1987.

Your Excellency, Lord.

I have the honour to address you to submit for your consideration and that of your Government a suggestion regarding the improvement of the Fluvial Network of the River Plate, which I will briefly present:

The great floods that ravage vast riverine territories almost annually to the great platense rivers are caused, in part, by the enormous mass of water that the Parana drags into its entrance in the Argentine plain.

Precisely in the area where the Parana enters the plain, the course of Uruguay runs at a distance of approximately 100 kilometres. The courses of both rivers were united in another geological age and now they are separated by a flat plain. Below, the Uruguay River channel is wide, well constituted, capable of receiving a much larger volume of water than it currently carries.

The proposal we make is to retain the waters of the Parana in the outskirts of Posadas and divert them through a channel - which would be supported by the Mountain Range of

Missions - to the Uruguay River channel.

This would result in the following results:

The Alto Parana would be regulated, no longer flooding the low plains.

The riverbed of the Parana from Posadas to the sea, that is, the one that the river has excavated in the Pampas plain, could be cultivated in the same way as the Nile Valley in Egypt, either by rain crops or with the waters of Paraná itself -Paraguay during the dry season.

The waters of Paraguay and those that should pass through the Posadas dike would continue to flow through the lower Parana, so that the navigability of the river ports would be assured.

The alveus of the main body of water, the channel of Uruguay would become navigable and would serve as direct communication, shorter than that of Parana to southwestern Brazil.

This is the suggestion that I am pleased to direct you, in case it has not been contemplated so far in the development projects of your great country.

Yours sincerely,

Juan Sanz Sanz"

Use of the Atlantic Rivers of the Iberian Peninsula

1984

SYNOPSIS:

The future of the Spanish economy is only in the development of the only firm resource it has: agriculture. But this development cannot be natural, because the current possibilities are little less than exhausted. It is necessary to introduce a new element, and this cannot be other than the systematic application of large-scale irrigation, through an exhaustive use of water resources.

All this revolves around the possible execution of the project designed to take advantage of the

waters of the Atlantic rivers of the Iberian Peninsula for the irrigation of the southern plains.

<u>Territory:</u>

The Minyo has a flow at the mouth of 350 m3; the Duero, 600 m3: the Mondego, 180 m3; the Tagus, 500 m3; the Guadiana, 80 m3; the Guadalquivir, 200 m3. Total 1,910 m3. Adding the flow of other coastal rivers of Galicia and Portugal, no less than 2,000 m3, as much as the Nile. The project is to create a vast system of irrigation along the Atlantic coast, from Galicia to the thirsty lands of the South.

As the Peninsula is very mountainous, rivers often approach the sea encased in narrow valleys. On the other hand, coastal saws cut the coastal plains. To drive the water southward there will be no choice but to cut some of these saws through considerable engineering works.

The most difficult of these projects is between the Minyo and the Duero, where there is hardly any coastal plain and the mountains reach the sea. This would force to do without the Minyo, the Limia, the Cávado and the Ave, before arriving at the Duero, which is the starting point. In this way, the usable water flow would be 1,600 m3. This water flow is sufficient, in principle. If more water were needed later, that of the Galician rivers and that of Beira al N. del Duero could be collected. It's about taking the Duero as a starting point. Successively, the waters of the Duero, Vouga, Mondego, Tagus, Sado, etc.

A large canal would have to collect the entire waters of the Duero at a height of 100 ms, for example, which will be the level at which it must be maintained. A first reservoir, just above Porto. Immediately to the

S the first irrigated strip would begin, in the Beira Litoral, between the mouth of the Duero and the Cavoeiro cape, triangular in shape, 150 x 50 km, 4,000 km2.

Once this plain has been irrigated, it is necessary to cross the low mountain ranges that separate it from the Tagus, which some sites have just over 200 ms. so that the ditch would not be very expensive. Large areas of the Ribatejo, in the surroundings of Lisbon could be watered next and, more to the S, also large spaces of the Lower Alemtejo, in the Sado valley. Here posible a 10,000 km2 space would be irrigated.

The passage between the Sado and the Guadiana is not too difficult either and through this river, which has hardly any territories to benefit, you enter the Betic plain, whose lowlands less than 100 ms, reach Cordoba. A triangle between Ayamonte and Tarifa (200 km) with 150 km inland, 15,000 km2 in total. Thus, directly, the canal would irrigate 30,000 km2 of Mediterranean irrigation, with several harvests per year or high yield plantation crops. In addition, along the southern coast, water could be taken to all coastal Las Vegas, Malaga, Granada, Almeria, and even Murcia and Alicante.

The climate of the southern plains that are intended to irrigate is fully in the subtropical climate, which is characterized by the lack of frost, but with mild winter temperatures, close to the cold. This climate is very specific: a prolonged warm season, with constant temperatures above zero, and a cool season, without frost. In the case of a transition between the climate called temperate -which is cold for us- and the always warm climate, both plants in one and another area thrive in it.

<u>**Considerations:**</u>

The problem of the economic development of a country is quite complicated. There are endless limitations. First, the resources; then, the financial and human resources available; Finally, the competition of the remaining States, within the country and in the international market. However, economic activity is like a cycle, in which some factors arouse others, chaining each other, so that the cycle cannot develop if a link is missing or if it is too weak and can break somewhere. The domestic market and the world market are the objectives of economic activity. Placing products in the hands of the buyer is the purpose of the economic activity. It may be an excessively mercantilist vision, but the mission is not to ensure the minimum needs alone.

In the specific case of Spain, the matter must be analysed based on the principle, that is, on the resources available. These basic resources are agricultural, mining and energy. You can also count as a resource what exists already done, that is, the entire industrial infrastructure. This is also a resource, as it is a starting point from which you can start.

Spanish mining resources are quite mediocre, lacking precisely the main raw materials. That is, there are these mineral raw materials, but to a mediocre extent, insufficient for the industry. We are lacking in iron, copper, bauxite. We have some important minerals, such as lead, some tin, mercury, pyrites. Except for pyrites, mercury and perhaps lead, otherwise, Spanish mining is lacking. The possibilities of increasing production of these mines are not great either. So, by this way little is possible to do.

As for energy resources, the possibilities are even more limited. We completely lack the basic energy source of this era: hydrocarbons. We only have some coal, unprofitable, and hydroelectric power. Hydroelectric production could increase a little more, but not much. So in this area the resources are also quite poor.

Finally, we find all the industrial and financial infrastructure - accumulation of tools and capital. It corresponds to the level of our current economy; that is, mediocre, without great possibilities of rapid expansion.

Thus, we come to agricultural resources. This is the specific field in which the possibilities of expansion are greater, because in it the Spanish economy has a great advantage: the Mediterranean climate. Spain is the country in the world that has greater extensions of this specific climate, in which a set of special productions are developed. In addition, subtropical and boreal productions are possible in this climate.

With the entry into the EEC (The author wrote it in 1984, Spain has to undergo a series of specific productions) within it; that is to say, to the products that are also obtained in the remaining community agriculture, but not to those in which we do not compete; for example, cotton, citrus, surely corn. That is, in those productions that the EEC imports. This is the issue that could be thoroughly analysed, because this would be the way to lay a firm economic base.

Let us not forget that within the community, Denmark and Ireland are two States that depend fundamentally on agricultural activity, not industrial activity. The economic path for Portugal and Spain is the same, not only for the community market, but because their productions cannot harm the balance of European agriculture.

The future of the Spanish economy is only in the development of the only firm resource it has: agriculture. But this development cannot be natural, because the current possibilities are little less than exhausted. It is necessary to introduce a new element, and this cannot be other than the systematic application of large-scale irrigation, through an exhaustive use of water resources. All this revolves around the possible execution of the project designed to take advantage of the waters of the Atlantic rivers of the Iberian Peninsula for the irrigation of the southern plains.

The plains of the Ribatejo and Alemtejo, of the Betica, could be great oases, of the Egyptian style, but larger. The amount of water carried by the Spanish rivers is higher than that of the Nile. This is the basis on which the Spanish economy could evolve steadily.

The Spanish economy leads an extremely inert existence, reflects European activity and, in a way, parasitic. Abroad, the survival of our economy is frequently negotiated on political, military and cultural arguments, rather than economic. But these arguments, in case of generalized economic crisis, may not be heard and our economy, lacking a firm base, would soon enter into a sharp bankruptcy (* 1984). Spain needs a firmer base on which to stand than mere conjunctural agreements. Being in the EEC is a guarantee, in part, of survival, but it is not a total guarantee. The Spanish economy must support itself, if possible; if it is not, there is no doubt that nothing can be done other than what is done.

Hence, a solution is proposed that may have been raised previously, but which can contribute to giving the Spanish economy a firmer base than it currently has.

PROPOSAL:

"December 9, 1984.
Sir:
I have the place to address you with a proposal regarding the use of the hydraulic resources of the Iberian Atlantic rivers in the irrigation of the southern plains, which in summary consists of the following:

The Atlantic rivers of the Peninsula have a considerable flow (350 m3 / s the Minyo, 100 m3 / s the Limia, 600 m3 / s the Duero, 180 m3 / s the Mondego, 500 m3 / s the Tagus). Together, more than 1,500 m3 / s. Due to lack of agricultural space and climatic conditions, it is barely possible to take advantage of them for optimal irrigation.

On the contrary, in the southern part of the Iberian Peninsula there are large flat or semi-flat spaces - Alemtejo, Betica-, territories lacking water, whose rivers run a relatively small flow. They are two complementary factors. In the North, the water is left over and cannot be used, while in the South this water, if it existed, would bear splendid fruits.

The proposal or suggestion that I allow myself to direct to your Government is to unite these two complementary factors, taking this northern water to the great southern plains, by constructing a canal that, by the height of approximately 100 meters, collects the waters of the Duero, and, through the Beira Litoral, those of Mondego and Vouga; cross the slopes that limit the north of the Tagus estuary, low altitude, cross the Alemtejo peneplains, also low altitude, reach the Lower Guadiana and reach the plains. Almost all the cultivable space located below 100 meters above the sea could be irrigated.

If the amount of water that could be drifted southward was 1,000 to 1,200 cubic meters per second, 2 or 3 million hectares could be irrigated.

It is a considerable work, but technically feasible, and its economic results would generously compensate for the effort. Spain would have a very firm agrarian base.

The warm climate of the territories that could be irrigated would allow the development of subtropical productions of which Europe is deficient, so that this production would not cause a conflict with the current European agrarian system.

On the other hand, the need for Portugal and Spain to participate jointly in the realization of this company would cause a close interdependence between the two States, which would end the traditional isolation of both peoples.

Hoping that the ideas presented are useful, he greets you very cordially,

Juan Sanz Sanz"

Indochina
1983

SYNOPSIS:

The cultivation of the vast lowland area of Southern Indochina is the main objective of this project. Take advantage of the waters of the northern half of the subcontinent, mountainous and heavy rains, to irrigate its southern half. The key to the project is the regularization of the waters of the Mekong, a river that has a flow of 13,000 meters 3 / second at the mouth.

For that it would be necessary to build two large reservoirs. One at the exit of the river from the mountains, which retains the waters of the entire upper course. The most appropriate point seems to be immediately above Luang Prabang. With the waters retained here, the plains of East Thailand and the Menam Valley could be irrigated. A second reservoir at the exit of the river to the coastal plain, in the region of the falls, to regularize the lower course and irrigate Cambodia and Cochinchina.

Complementary to the Mekong project are those of Iravadi and the Red River of Tonkin, Cambodia and Cochinchina. The same work is necessary in the Tonkin and Annam rivers. But there is a very special project in this region, around the use of the Saluen River.

THE INDOCHINA PROBLEM:

<u>Ideas for a subcontinent transformation project.</u>

One.

Indochina's problem is particularly delicate, not only because of the conflicts that occur there, but because world peace is truly threatened by this situation of chronic belligerence. We are faced with a phenomenon of balkanization. With a set of states in precarious equilibrium, with serious reasons for potential conflict and confronted on different sides, behind which are much greater powers.

Apparently, the danger that a local conflict will generalize and may acquire global dimensions is greater in Western Asia, Central America, or in places of permanent tension such as Central Europe. But, precisely because of this, the risk is in minor practice, because the pacifist will that undoubtedly exists today in the world is pending of them and puts all the effort into preventing them from growing.

The Indochina conflict, on the other hand, is apparently less important, less peremptory. Far from the areas of immediate interests of the great military or industrial powers, it does not seem to threaten directly more than those concerned. For this reason, in part, this conflict has become perennial, it seems to have no end. But in this fact lies precisely the great danger, because a chronic conflict, if it finds new reasons for discord to feed itself and, in turn, does not find the pacifist will sufficiently informed and cautious, can reach an unpredictable outcome.

Remember how World War I began, after a long period of peace of almost half a century. The bloody contest on the frontier of the great belligerent powers was not unleashed, but in the most unexpected place. A local conflict that dragged intermediate powers, which, in turn, pushed the elders into it. In Indochina the same phenomenon of balkanization occurs and what happened then could be repeated in the future.

This subcontinent lives a situation of belligerence, to a greater or lesser extent, constant for more than forty years (* 1983). These conflicts exist by themselves and, in part, by the influence of external factors. But new elements of discord are beginning to come into play, which will aggravate their virulence. And it is here precisely where there is the danger of them becoming more than a distant war, which does not endanger the great world interests.

Two.

In a somewhat arbitrary way the world was divided into continents and it would be more appropriate to do it in smaller geographical spaces, which form an inner world, a microcosm, in which the societies that live in them have more relationship and affinity with each other than with bordering, which form, in turn, another peculiar area, another microcosm. This community that arouses an inevitable coexistence is caused by a certain geographical determinism. Thus, in Asia, the space of Iran and the Turan form a natural unity; also, the Indian space or the Chinese space. In Southeast Asia we find two subcontinents: Indochina and Insulindia. Although both are usually included in this general meaning of "Southeast Asia", the reality is that they form two completely different organisms. While Insulindia is a vast maritime space, in which all the villages live close to the sea and almost all relations are carried out through it, in the Indochinese space we find societies, usually interiors, with their backs to the sea, except on the Vietnamese coast. Indochina is a closed world, of terrestrial roads, of little navigable rivers, surrounded by coastal mountain ranges, jungle, that isolate from the outside, with small alluvial basins separated by wild and uninhabited spaces and, also, subjected to the constant pressure of a vast territory Northern mountain that is also part of it. In turn, the great navigation routes are removed from the Indo-Chinese world by that long arm that is the Malacca Peninsula, as if nature is not enough barriers that for the penetration of other cultures are its jungle mountains and its habitable nuclei isolated.

Indochinese space comprises, not only the peninsula itself - from which Malaysia must be separated - but the vast mountainous region that extends to the North and reaches the confines of Tibet: the Yunnan and part of the Kuangsi. These territories have been politically integrated into China for centuries, whose binding capacity has reached this point. But in previous times they gravitated towards the South, forming a natural community with the societies of the southern valleys. This does not mean anything from a political point of view, since politics is overcoming these natural limitations and it is always beneficial that, within borders of the State, which do not have to correspond with the geographical ones, different societies live together and enrich each other's cultures. But this northern mountainous space, which is part of the Indochinese microcosm, is one of the strangest regions in the world. A bundle of large parallel rivers, encased in deep and insane chasms and separated by high jungle mountains, has formed an impassable barrier throughout history for the relationship between the two great cultures of that part of the world: India and China. Between Bengal and Sechuan, two territories to which the high civilization arrived thousands of years ago, there are only a thousand kilometres in a straight line through this mountainous jungle. However, these cultures have not been able to shake hands through it. On the contrary, they have had to follow the sea route, several times longer, or make a huge detour through the steppes of Central Asia. On this last path, Buddhism arrived in China.

Thus, we have that on the habitable core of Indochina in the great southern valleys - Iravadi, Menam, Mekong, Red - they have gravitated, over time, two types of opposite influences. An external influence for the superior cultures of China and India, which it has found to take root the difficulties that Nature presents and have only been able to penetrate from the sea through the scarce low and open spaces of the mouths of these great rivers. Actually, the influence of these higher cultures has been realized by land, through a long road that goes from Bengal to South China, passing through Burma, Thailand, Cambodia, Annam and Tonkin. And in the face of this influence of higher cultures, counteracting it, there is the action of mountain peoples, semi-savages, who once and again have descended to the low plains at a time when societies created in densely populated valleys, reflective culture , they were in crisis.

We are faced with a hermetic natural space, divided into watertight compartments, subjected to the action, on the one hand, of civilizations from abroad, which arouse reflex cultures; and, on the other, of semi-wild mountain villages that have caused a society to be rejuvenated during the times when culture had degenerated. This is what it has been in the past and what we find today is nothing but, to a large extent, its result. Indochina has seen different cultures pass through its soil over the millennia, but she herself remains unchanged, hermetic, with one foot in the highest civilization and another in radical primitivism. Do not be dazzled by the wonders of Angkor; This is only one side of the coin.

Three.

On this background that the past bequests us and that conditions the future is the present situation. As in the rest of the Third World countries, there is a factor that is totally shocking national societies, forcing them to transform radically: population growth. The number of inhabitants that coexist in a society is one of the determining factors of its structure. If this number varies significantly, multiplying several times, the structure of society varies as well. It is a quantitative factor that ends up producing qualitative effects. If we take the example of Thailand, we see that a little over a century ago its territory was home to some 6 million people, which today have become almost 50 (* 1983); that is, the number of its inhabitants has been multiplied by 8. This vertiginous growth is a formidable driving force, which prevents society from remaining static and forces it to transform. As Thailand is a country of the extension of Spain or France, it was able to feed many more inhabitants than it had in the not too distant past. But it is reaching - and this example applies to other countries in the area - a critical situation in which the subsistence capacity is reached the limit bearable with the current means. Not long-ago Thailand, Burma and Vietnam were among the main rice exporters. The large plantations of the Iravadi, Menam and Mekong deltas were created for this commercial purpose.

Today these countries need most of their food resources for their own subsistence. All of them depend heavily on foreign aid. None have a solid economy, which guarantees their stability. Meanwhile, the demographic factor and, in turn, the widespread desire of the mass to share the goods of a modern standard of living continue to push forward.

On the other hand, someone might think that war, with its death, is a remedy against this population growth and against the hope of the mass to improve their living conditions. In some warm minds this possibility appears from time to time. But it is something that precisely in this part of the world has proved completely false. In Cambodia, the successive calamities caused a terrible disappearance of the population of manhood. And yet, population growth has not only remained large, but has compensated for those losses.

The population can only regulate its growth by itself, not by the intervention of external factors. One of the causes that the number of inhabitants has grown so much in recent generations has been the disappearance of the great epidemics, which previously decimated it. But the real cause of population growth in tropical countries is economic. Indeed, the cultivation systems of those countries, especially those that base their subsistence on the cultivation of rice, require collaboration in the agricultural work of children, who perform lighter, but necessary, work that would otherwise be make a man. The exploitation system that exists there today is based on this fact. Child labour is necessary, at the family level, to move forward. There are many children because parents need them to grow their small farms.

Only an economic and, therefore, social change can make this population regulate spontaneously. As long as the step is not taken in front of mechanizing and electrifying the countryside and making rural farms sufficient for the maintenance of families, this dizzying population growth will be inevitable. This problem is all the more serious because in our time a situation has been reached in which, with the current means, the food capacity of those countries has reached the limit. Traditional systems of exploitation and cultivation, despite the improvements that have been gradually introduced, do not give for more. The situation needs to change.

Four.

In tropical countries, agriculture is the primary economic activity. It produces most of the income and employs a large majority of the population. From our western perspective, from industrialized countries, we do not repair this fact. But the great masses of the Third World subsist, for the most part, thanks to the exploitation of the land, either in the form of agriculture almost exclusively in Asian countries, well associated with large-scale livestock as in America. That is why, being agriculture its main source of wealth, it is also its biggest problem.

Tropical agriculture is the result of the great rains that fall in these regions, the wettest in the world. At a great distance, it is the part of the world where it rains the most. Fighting against the primitive jungle, the peasant has managed to cultivate those territories where the force of Nature was less powerful: spaces of clear forest, without stagnant waters, with good river or sea communications, enriched by river silts, but these rains are very irregular; Variations from one year to another are from 1 to 3 or from 1 to 4, with great extremes of floods and devastating droughts. In most of the countries that are not around the equator, they only occur during one season, which is cultivation, while the other half of the year suffers from a persistent drought. However, the rains during the monsoon season do not always fall with the same intensity or in the same places. It is enough that for ten days the rains do not make their appearance on the crops, in the rainy season, so that these grow, and the harvest is lost. However, if the rains are sufficient and arrive on time, any tilled land gives remarkable yields, with hardly any need for fertilizers, only with human labour. But this only happens less often. Normally, there are large variations in crop yields, with its sequels of years of abundance and shortage.

Where there are two rainy seasons - countries around the equator, Central China, Northwest India - two crops can be obtained.

But almost all tropical territories have no more than a single wet season and, therefore. A single harvest.

This is the situation that must be corrected and for this there is no other solution than to generalize crops by irrigation, that is, to take advantage of the water of the rivers. Trade winds and monsoons ensue with extreme violence, flooding the fields and swelling the rivers. The tropical rivers have a very irregular flow, with variations ranging from 1 to 100 between runoff and flood. Its main mission is to serve as a drain to the general flood. Mediocre waterways, despite their flow, are only useful during the flood. They pass by the cultivated fields with the rains as undesirable foreigners, of which we must defend themselves by strong dikes, like Damocles sword that hangs over the countryside, to which devastate the smallest weakness of the retaining walls.

This residual water from the rains that the rivers will lose in the sea is the one that should be used exhaustively through irrigation. This would compensate for the irregularity of the rains, obtain a second crop during the dry season and earn large areas that are not cultivated today due to lack of water. For this it is necessary to regularize the rivers, by means of reservoirs, retaining the waters of the rainy season to use them in the dry season. This regularization would bring two notable consequences, in addition. On the one hand, avoid the great flooding of the rivers in the low alluvial lands, which are the most fertile, where the levees fail to prevent it. And provide these countries with a source of electrical energy that serves as a basis for their industrial development.

Five.

In the specific case of Indochina, everything said in the previous point can be applied here. Heavy rains at the headwaters of the rivers and on the coast; a much less rainy central nucleus, which reaches steppe in some regions. Extensive mountainous countries in the North and along the coast and vast plains in the center and along the valleys. Rain crops in the deltas of the great rivers -Iravadi, Menam. Mekong, Red- , protected by dikes. Extensive low regions that flood during the summer flood. Discontinuous population. The four great deltas are the vital centres of the subcontinent, On the Annamita coast, along the Mekong, the upper Menam, the middle Iravadi, small isolated bottom. And the tropical forest always present, enveloping the inhabited nuclei.

The cultivation of the vast lowland area of Southern Indochina is the main objective of this project. Take advantage of the waters of the northern half of the subcontinent, mountainous and heavy rains, to irrigate its southern half. The key to the project is the regularization of the waters of the Mekong, a river that has a flow of 13,000 meters 3 / second at the mouth. For that it would be necessary to build two large reservoirs. One at the exit of the river from the mountains, which retains the waters of the entire upper course. The most appropriate point seems to be immediately above Luang Prabang. With the waters retained here, the plains of East Thailand and the Menam Valley could be irrigated. A second reservoir at the exit of the river to the coastal plain, in the region of the falls, to regularize the lower course and irrigate Cambodia and Cochinchina. Each one should have a capacity of approximately 150 km3. From these two points the waters can be easily distributed by channels on their respective low plains.

The Menam Valley, the plain of Thailand itself, could thus be completely irrigated. Today only its southern half is used, since the northern one is turned into a swamp, a natural pond that retains the waters and is uninhabited. It would be necessary to deepen the channel of the Menam so that these swamps would disappear and irrigate the plains with waters of the Mekong coming from the upper pond or from the lower one through Cambodia.

The plains of East Thailand, inhabited mainly by Laotians, are not very fertile as a whole and partly covered with swamps. It would be necessary to facilitate its drainage towards the Mekong, towards the lower reservoir of this river. Although the lands are not too fertile, perhaps the cultivation by irrigation it would make them profitable.

The low plains of Cambodia would no longer be flooded and could be fully utilized. Now less than a fifth of the territory is cultivated. As for the Mekong Delta, which is a marked dry season, it could yield two crops and double its current yield.

Once the Mekong was regulated, all the plains of South Indochina would see their harvest assured

During the monsoon season, compensating for the irregularity of the rains. The extension of cultivated land would be expanded, multiplying several times. And a second crop would be achieved in the lands that are under cultivation.

Six.

Complementary to the Mekong project are those of Iravadi and the Tonkin Red River. The Iravadi is a very large river (13,000 m3 / s) that runs through a low and relatively narrow valley, with heavy rainfall at the head and in the delta and a fairly dry central region. It is navigable to Bhamo, 1,600 kilometres from the sea. Near this point the waters of the upper part should be retained. A little further down, in Mandalay, its width in runoff is 2 kilometres and 12 in flood. This gives us an idea of the amount of water that could be used. With it the aims pointed out above would be achieved: avoid disastrous floods, compensate for the irregularity of rainfall in the less favoured years, obtain a second crop during the dry season and, finally, extend the crop area. We can assume what this would mean for Burma.

The same work is necessary in the Tonkin and Annam rivers. The chief of them, the Red, periodically devastated the low plain. Its waters would give a second harvest. Also the small valleys of the rivers of the Annamita coast need artificial irrigation, despite the abundance of rainfall and the double season in which they occur. But their basins are extremely overcrowded and what they produce is not enough.

Seven.

Until now the renewal of the fertility of the fields has been produced by flood silt or organic fertilizer. Putting so many new lands under cultivation and submitting to those that already exist for intensive exploitation, with two or more harvests per year, requires the massive use of chemical fertilizers. This means increasing the cost of exploitation; but it is inevitable and would be more than compensated by the increase in production in general and yields per hectare.

Some countries that today do not produce what is necessary for sufficient food, if their cultivated areas were extended and their crops increased in yield through the systematic application of irrigation, they would not only have superabundant food, with which to cope with rapid population growth , but they could devote a part of the effort to the production of agricultural raw materials for the industry - textiles, oilseeds - and commercial plantations. We know that in the current situation of saturation of the world market and of falling prices of these products this is something unthinkable and utopian. But we believe that projects have to be done towards a general improvement in living standards and an increase in trade. The material level of civilizations is determined by the intensity of trade. Society can only move forward in this direction and, if it does not, it goes back and ends up becoming atomized. This is the way for civilization to become impoverished and end up disintegrating. A level of full civilization is one in which products from everywhere reach everywhere. You cannot move backwards; restrictive policies cannot produce anything other than general ruin.

Eight.

On the other hand, man does not live on bread alone - as they say. Large reservoirs would also be sources of energy with which to electrify those countries, giving it the basis for its urban and industrial development. One of the biggest problems suffered by the region is the lack of energy sources, since neither oil, coal nor natural gas are obtained in appreciable quantities. This base is as necessary as the agricultural one. Agriculture and energy are the two feet on which those societies could start.

But there is a very special project in this region, around the use of the Saluen River. This river has no agricultural utility. It runs entirely through a deep groove, hundreds and even thousands of meters below the mountains, until its very exit to the sea. It seems as if he wanted to go unnoticed. However, it crosses very rainy regions and its flow seems to be 10,000 meters3 / second. Its water today is useless and before the contrary, the chasm through which it flows, unhealthy and covered with thick jungle, has been the biggest obstacle that travellers found on the shortest path between India and China. Their mouths are located about 150 kilometres east of Rangun. A hundred kilometres from the mouth could be built a hydroelectric station, which could be made as high as one would like, since the mountains that fall at the peak of the river are more than 1,000 meters. Recall that the Rogunsky and Nurek dams, both on land, are 488 and 317 meters high respectively. This dike would be a work certainly colossal. If it were possible to give it a height of, for example, 500 meters, its annual electricity production capacity would be 400,000 million kilowatt hours, five times more than the Itapu dam, on the Paraná, recently completed. The proximity of the sea, the railway between Rangun and Moulmein and the ports of both cities - the latter is in its estuary - would facilitate the works. With only that dam, Indochina could be electrified, provided that the flow attributed to it is 10,000 meters3 / second.

Nine.

It is necessary to provoke a general improvement in Indochina, by this procedure or another similar one, that faces the problem that represents the vertiginous growth of the population and the growing demand for a better standard of living that exists today in the masses, but, above all , it is necessary to face a difficult political problem. Politics only deals with the necessary things, not with what can be good or optimal. This project is not only a benefit for those countries, but a necessity for global stability, for the reasons we pointed out in the first point of this study.

Indeed, in Indochina two heavily armed states, Thailand and Vietnam, each clearly aligned with a military bloc. In turn, around the region, two military powers - China and India - that we can describe as intermediate since, despite their power, they are far from the major ones. And all this revolving around the internal situation of the subcontinent, which we have already seen what it is. It is necessary that this situation change, that internal, local, discord motives disappear, to prevent the danger that a turbulent situation, over time, can trigger a much greater conflict, of incalculable proportions. It is a conflict that is there, it is a problem that needs to be resolved. The construction of five large reservoirs and a few irrigation channels is not an excessive price and the international community must, by this means or another, preserve its survival.

STUDY:

"April, 1983.

Mr. president.

In response to the appeal that the North-South Commission made to public opinion last February and taking advantage of the intellectual hospitality it provides, I send you a study on the problems of Indochina, which I hope can be useful in the work of that commission to clarify ideas and outline solutions.

Waiting for it, receive a cordial greeting.

Juan Sanz Sanz"